HYPNOSIS AND HYPNOTHERAPY

HYPNOSIS
&
HYPNOTHERAPY
David T. Rowley

CROOM HELM
London & Sydney

THE CHARLES PRESS, PUBLISHERS
Philadelphia

© 1986 David T. Rowley
Croom Helm Ltd, Provident House, Burrell Row,
Beckenham, Kent, BR3 1AT
Croom Helm Australia Pty Ltd, Suite 4, 6th Floor,
64-76 Kippax Street, Surry Hills, NSW 2010, Australia

British Library Cataloguing in Publication Data

Rowley, David T.
    Hypnosis and hypnotherapy.
    1. Hypnotism   2. Hypnotism — Therapeutic
use
    I. Title
    154.7   BF1141

    ISBN 0-7099-2257-4
    ISBN 0-7099-2271-X Pbk

and
The Charles Press, Publishers, PO Box 15715
Philadelphia, Pennsylvania 19103

Library of Congress Catalog Card Number
86-7123

ISBN 0-914783-13-0 (cl)
ISBN 0-914783-15-7 (p)

Printed and bound in Great Britain by Mackays of Chatham Ltd, Kent

CONTENTS

Preface
Acknowledgements

To Mother and Father, for helping to make this book possible. Thank you.

PREFACE

When I started writing this book I meant it as a guide; something for interested individuals to read to help them find their way around the ever-growing area of hypnosis. I continue to hope that it fulfils that aim, and rather like a map guides the reader deftly through the torturous terrain of hypnosis. It was not my intention to intrude personally into this book, but rather to be non-interpretive in my approach, favouring neither one theory nor the other.

However, as the reader will discover, I very soon found this to be impossible. The act of writing distils and refines knowledge, but it also adds to it. It seemed to me that in several areas a summary of the research was simply not adequate, rather it was necessary to take sides, and even on occasions to reinterpret research findings and propose new research strategies and hypotheses. This explains partly why each chapter ends with a section entitled 'Personal Reflections', although I confess I have not limited myself to this section when it comes to putting forward my own thoughts.

This book is really written for students and professionals who are interested in hypnosis, but would like to know more. There seems to be quite an increase in the use of hypnosis within the Health Service in the United Kingdom, and I would hope this book will provide an introduction for those professionals who are considering using this technique. I hope it also has something to offer to those whose knowledge of hypnosis is rather more profound.

I approached hypnosis as a cognitive psychologist interested in therapy, and I suspect this shows in the book I have written. I believe most strongly that one must be cautious in discussing the therapeutic uses of hypnosis, anything else would be disastrous. There are still those around who believe that hypnosis is a magical, mystical phenomenon of great potential danger, and would greatly restrict its use. I recommend this book to them, providing they are prepared to give up such views.

One last comment. The alternative title of this book is 'The Phenomenon of Hypnosis and Its Therapeutic Applications'. Its actual title means the same thing, to me if to no-one else.

Dave Rowley

ACKNOWLEDGEMENTS

There are many people who have helped bring this book to fruition; to any whose names I omit, my sincere apologies.
For conversations, and for convincing me of the worth of personal testimony, Dave Hiles.
For support and good humour, Harry Purser and Chris Code.
For making a stand, Pam Grunwell.
For useful comments and difficult questions (and for being good subjects) the students of the School of Speech Pathology, Leicester Polytechnic.
For technical support, Olivetti, Micropro, Hewlett Packard and the staff of the Computer Centre, Leicester Polytechnic.
For patience, Tim Hardwick.
For understanding, you, the reader.
And most of all, for putting up with disgruntlement, disarray and simply not being there, my family; Christabel, Darcy and Leilah.

Chapter One

THE HISTORY OF HYPNOSIS

The history of hypnosis is the history of a struggle
for public acceptance, and for recognition as a
subject worthy of scientific investigation.
Throughout this history hypnotists have been
persecuted and ridiculed, often by their
contemporaries in the medical profession. Despite
these individual setbacks however, hypnosis itself
has progressed steadily, so that today it is the
subject of scientific study and is highly valued as
an adjunct to therapy.
Many books commence with a chapter devoted to
an historical overview of hypnosis. One reason for
this is that the history of hypnosis is really
quite fascinating, populated by some rather
colourful and charismatic individuals, Franz Mesmer
being the best known. Furthermore, it is interesting
that the ways in which hypnotized individuals act
often mirror the prevailing views about hypnosis at
a particular period in its history. Without an
historical perspective it is not so easy to
understand the current controversies surrounding
hypnosis and its use, for although hypnotists are no
longer persecuted, there are still quite a number of
misconceptions about hypnosis, which this book will
attempt to remove.
Hypnosis has a long history, going back at
least to the time of the Ancient Greeks and
Egyptians, and probably even further. Both the
Ancient Greeks and Egyptians had dream incubation
centres, where people came to receive guidance for
their problems. The purpose of these centres, as
their name suggests, was to induce dreams, and to do
this several techniques were used, including
fasting, praying and something akin to hypnotic
induction. These dreams were then reported to the
priests who provided interpretations which it was

1

hoped would suggest a solution to the problem.
    In addition, Miller (1979) reports that in both
countries hypnotic suggestion was also used. In
Ancient Greece people were treated in 'Sleep Temples
of the Sick'. Here sleep was induced by a
combination of methods, including music, drugs and
repetitious speech. In Egypt 'Temple Sleep' was
induced by incense and chanting, and during the
resulting state suggestions were made that the
symptoms would disappear and the patient would be
cured.
    The history of 'modern' hypnosis is often
thought to begin with Mesmer in the last quarter of
the eighteenth century. However, there are two
important forerunners of Mesmer who merit a brief
mention. They are Paracelsus (1493-1541) and Van
Helmont (1577-1644). Paracelsus was a Swiss
physician who believed that the stars influence
human beings through magnetism, and that all magnets
have an effect on humans. Van Helmont took this idea
further, and proposed that each person radiated
'animal magnetism' which could influence both the
minds and bodies of others. This idea has developed
since then into the laying on of hands used by faith
healers, although any cure which results is now
attributed to God's power rather than animal
magnetism.

FRANZ MESMER

The scene was then ready for Friedrich (Franz) Anton
Mesmer (1734-1815). Mesmer was born at Iznang on
Lake Constance. As a young man he read widely,
studying theology, philosophy and law before gaining
his medical degree in 1776. The thesis he submitted
for his doctorate dealt with the possibility of the
stars and planets influencing curative powers.
Mesmer's thesis indicated his growing interest in
the curative powers of magnets, which probably
stemmed from his earlier contact with Father
Maximilian Hell (1720-1792), a Viennese Jesuit. It
was Father Hell who gave Mesmer some magnets to
experiment with, and as a result of these
experiments he concluded that to be healthy an
individual must be in electro-chemical equilibrium
with the stars and planets. If this equilibrium is
disturbed ill-health will result, but equilibrium,
and therefore good health, can be restored by using
magnets.
    Shortly after attaining his medical degree

2

Mesmer began practising medicine. He was an ambitious and charismatic individual, eager to be accepted by Viennese society. This desire was fulfilled when he married Anna Von Bosch, the wealthy widow of an officer of the Austrian Imperial Army. However, his professional life was not proceeding as smoothly as his social life.

In one way Mesmer was perhaps too successful. He was able to induce trances with great ease, and often appeared to produce miraculous cures. Of course, as his fame grew the trances and the cures became still easier to achieve. However, his success was not to the liking of many of his professional colleagues, partly because of the unscientific nature of his methods, and partly because of professional envy. A little later their chance came to denounce Mesmer, although almost until the end it seemed as if it would be one of Mesmer's greatest successes.

The event which led to Mesmer being discredited in Vienna began with a child called Maria Theresa Paradis going blind. However, Maria was no ordinary child, she was an exceptionally gifted pianist, and a protege of the Empress Maria Theresa. Mesmer was invited to attempt to cure the child. As far as it is possible to tell the case was one of hysterical blindness, so it is perhaps not too surprising that Mesmer was able to effect a cure. However, the matter did not end there, unfortunately for Mesmer. Maria's family worried that her pension from the Empress might end now that her sight was restored. Probably because of the emotional pressure she was under Maria's blindness returned, and her parents refused to let Mesmer see her again. Quite irrationally this cost Mesmer the favour of the Empress and many of her officials. His enemies in the medical profession seized their chance and denounced Mesmer as a fraud.

Mesmer quickly realized there was little future for him in Vienna, and in 1778 he left for Paris. He knew a number of people in Paris, and in addition he was fortunate enough to interest Dr. Charles d'Eslon in his treatment methods. Dr. d'Eslon was physician to the Comte d'Artois, who was the King's younger brother, so this was obviously a very useful contact for Mesmer. D'Eslon and Mesmer soon set up a joint clinic, which achieved great success. In fact it was so successful that Mesmer had to devise new methods to cope with all the potential patients, and his individual approach soon gave way to a group method of treatment.

The group therapy approach devised by Mesmer must admittedly have looked rather strange, but some modern group therapy techniques also look rather odd. Mesmer's patients entered a dimly lit, mirrored room complete with background music where they were confronted by a number of large oak vats. These vats contained water, iron filings and bottles. The patients were instructed to grasp the metal rods protruding from the bottles. Mesmer, dressed in lilac robes and waving a wand went from patient to patient, emphasizing the benefits of his treatment. As he came to each patient he would make passes over them with his hands, and perhaps touch them with magnets. Actually, probably without realizing it, Mesmer was employing a very powerful therapeutic technique. As the more suggestible of his patients responded to his words and chattered excitedly about the feelings they were experiencing they would influence their less suggestible neighbours, and hence there would be more likelihood of a cure.

Mesmer's goal was generally to get his patients to experience what was termed a crisis. This was very similar to what is now referred to as an hysterical reaction, and involved a convulsive reaction, which was usually accompanied by laughing, crying, and perhaps even unconsciousness. To produce a crisis of this kind is seldom the goal of modern therapeutic hypnosis. Thornton (1976) has argued that at least some of the patients Mesmer saw were suffering from epilepsy.

There is one other aspect of Mesmer's hypnotic technique which is worth revealing, since it gave rise to some enmity from both the Church and his professional colleagues. Most of Mesmer's patients were women, and often his induction techniques appeared to be overtly sexual. Mesmer liked to hold his patients' knees between his own, and this of course brought the lower parts of their bodies into close proximity. In addition Mesmer would sometimes stroke the lower part of the patient's abdomen.

Mesmer's patients often regarded him with awe and his method of treatment quickly became known as 'Mesmerism'. But once again, despite his apparent success, Mesmer also considered himself a conscientious medical practitioner and scientist. Consequently he was most upset when his findings were ignored by most of the scientific societies to which he sent them. Udolf (1981) reports a rumour that Mesmer was offered a large amount of money in exchange for his secret by the French Government, and that Mesmer refused this offer, as of course he

had to, since he possessed no real secret. Shortly
after this the King, Louis XVI, set up a Royal
Commission to investigate Mesmer. This task was
undertaken by the French Academy of Science in 1784.
On the Commission were a number of well known
scientists, including the discoverer of the
lightning rod, Benjamin Franklin, who happened to be
the American Ambassador to France at the time,
Lavoisier, the chemist, Jussieu, the botanist,
Bailly, the astronomer and Guillotin, the inventor
of the infamous instrument of execution. Despite the
presence of these famous individuals the
Commission's report appeared biased, and failed to
appreciate the significance of Mesmer's work. The
Commission's investigation took two main directions.
One was an investigation of Mesmer's past work, the
other was an investigation of the effect of magnets
on the Commission members themselves. They reported
that the magnets appeared to have no effect, and
that Mesmer's patients were not cured through the
use of magnets, but through Mesmer's suggestions
that they would be cured. Mesmer himself did not
demonstrate his methods to the Commission.
     The Commission concluded that magnets had no
effect on the patients, and hence that Mesmer's
methods were unscientific. Furthermore they stated
that Mesmer's methods may even be damaging to the
patient, citing some of Mesmer's failures as
examples, whilst largely ignoring his successes.
They also believed that the close contact between
the patient and Mesmer may have given rise to sexual
feelings and hence the treatment was immoral. It is
possible perhaps to excuse the Commission's report
on the grounds that the prevailing scientific views
of the time did not allow for concepts such as 'cure
by suggestion', but it is extremely disappointing
that they did not attach more weight to the
empirical evidence dealing with the large number of
patients who had benefited from his treatment.
     As a result of the Commission's investigations,
Mesmer's licence to practice was removed and he
retired to Versailles. Shortly before the French
revolution he left there to live in Frauenfeld in
Switzerland, on the shores of Lake Constance. While
there he treated the poor of the surrounding area,
and lived a relatively simple life. Three years
before his death in Meersburg on March the Fifth,
1815, he was invited to show his methods to the
Prussian Academy in Berlin. However, he refused the
invitation, perhaps because of his feelings of
bitterness.

Mesmer's importance in the establishment of hypnosis is immense. As a result of his work, many other practitioners took up his ideas and approaches, but paradoxically it was Mesmer's fame which brought about his downfall, and also a temporary lull in the use of hypnosis. Mesmer's downfall made it very difficult for individuals who wanted to investigate hypnosis to do so. They were unlikely to get any findings accepted, and might well fall foul of their medical organizations. However, a few individuals had recognized the importance of Mesmer's work, and continued it regardless, albeit with less flamboyance.

MARQUIS DE PUYSEGUR

The Marquis Armand de Puysegur (1751-1825) was a retired military man who became one of Mesmer's followers. He is particularly important in the history of hypnosis because of his recognition of the state he referred to as artificial somnambulism. This state is, from Puysegur's descriptions, much more akin to present concepts of the 'hypnotic trance'. In this state patients could open their eyes, walk about, speak, and respond to the mesmerist's wishes.

Puysegur and his followers also discovered that to bring about a 'crisis' was not necessary to cure the patient, as Mesmer appears to have thought, so this can be seen as a real breakthrough. Chertok (1981) in fact believes that Puysegur's approach was perhaps more complex than others of the nineteenth century. Typically the patient would be asked to verbalise his problem during the somnambulistic state, giving details about such things as its cause, symptoms, and outcome, and in turn receiving suggestions from the mesmerist. Here then can be seen the beginnings of many current treatment methods using hypnosis.

Puysegur's work also led to a reinterpretation of the theoretical foundations of Mesmerism. There was a move from the view that the mesmerist controlled a magnetic fluid which influenced the patient, to a belief that he directly controlled the patient by the power of his will. This was known as the doctrine of will power. It was believed that the mesmerist's brain secreted a fluid with curative powers which passed along the nerves to the peripheral organs, and then to the patient. The mesmerist controlled the secretion and flow of this fluid indirectly by the amount of confidence he possessed in the power of his will to dominate his patient. It is probably from this that one of the most common misconceptions of all concerning hypnosis stems: that the subject surrenders his will to the hypnotist.

Puysegur's therapy can thus be seen as very modern in comparison to his theoretical beliefs concerning the nature of hypnosis. This should not be taken as meaning that therapeutic methods employing hypnosis have stood still while theoretical ideas have advanced.

JOSE DI FARIA

Jose Custodi di Faria (1756-1819) arrived in Paris in 1814 from Goa, a Portuguese colony in India. His ideas were quite advanced, and he believed that somnambulism was produced by the subject's expectancy and receptivity, and that the effect of mesmeric passes, magnets, etc. was valuable only in so far as it increased expectancy and receptivity. As a result of this insight Faria concentrated on a verbal induction technique, in contrast to the previous mesmeric approaches.

JOHN ELLIOTSON

John Elliotson (1791-1868) was an English surgeon who began to use mesmerism in his work at University College in London, where he was chief staff physician and Professor of Surgery. In addition he defended Mesmer's theory of animal magnetism. However, Elliotson's professional colleagues were not in favour of his experiments with mesmerism, and the editor of the 'Lancet', Thomas Wakely, showed that Elliotson was in error in his belief that certain metals radiated more magnetic force and hence possessed greater curative powers. He was denounced as a fraud and forced to leave his post. However, he continued his work and stimulated others to carry out research in mesmerism, and was responsible for the founding of a journal called 'Zoist', which published articles on hypnosis.

JAMES BRAID

James Braid (1795-1860) was a surgeon in Manchester

who became interested in mesmerism after witnessing a demonstration of magnets by Lafontaine. At first Braid believed it to be a fake, but subsequent demonstrations of analgesia and eye catalepsy convinced him that the subject should be investigated further, as he could see the benefits of carrying out operations under hypnotically induced anaesthesia.

Braid believed that hypnosis was very closely related to sleep, and invented the term 'neurohypnology' (nervous sleep) to describe it, which was later shortened to 'hypnosis'. He falsely thought that hypnosis was brought about by fatigue of the eye muscles caused by long periods of fixation, and developed an induction technique based on this theory called Braidism. Although this technique is still used, it is the accompanying expectations and suggestions which are the real means of induction, not the eye fatigue.

As his investigations continued, Braid wanted to change the name of the trance state to 'monoideism', because of his view that hypnosis involves the subject concentrating on a single idea. However, by this time the name hypnosis was too well established. Braid also believed that the name neurohypnology (and hence its corruption, hypnosis) was inaccurate since he no longer thought of hypnosis as being akin to sleep. Braid was also one of the first persons to realize that there was no direct physiological link between the hypnotist and the subject which could be manipulated to induce hypnosis.

From the achievements mentioned above Braid can be seen as an important figure in the history of hypnosis. Although he did receive some criticism from the medical establishment, he was well respected and increased the medical acceptability of hypnosis by his conservative approach.

JAMES ESDAILE

James Esdaile (1808-1859) was, like Elliotson, interested in using hypnosis as an analgesic in surgery. While practising in India he read the work of Elliotson and Braid, and performed over three hundred operations using hypnosis. Most of these were for the removal of massive scrotal tumours, and he found that mortality rates dropped from 50 per cent to 5 per cent. Esdaile was keen to publish his findings, but with the exception of 'Zoist' the

medical journals did not reciprocate the wish.
Esdaile's work perhaps represents the first large scale use of hypnosis in surgical operations, and it is unfortunate that the advent of chemical anaesthetics led to a rapid decline in the use of hypnosis in this context, for there are some occasions, as will be seen later, when it can provide a useful alternative.

AMBROSE LIEBAULT

Ambrose August Liebault (1823-1904) was a French doctor who settled in Nancy in 1864. He was interested in hypnosis and discovered that by combining verbal suggestions of sleep with Braid's method of prolonged gaze, he was able to induce trances in 85 per cent of his patients. He published a book 'Du Sommeil' in 1866 which was ignored for twenty years until Hippolyte Bernheim, then Professor of Medicine at Strasbourg investigated Bernheim's work. (Perhaps Bernheim bought the only copy of 'Du Sommeil' reputedly sold).

HIPPOLYTE BERNHEIM

Hippolyte Marie Bernheim (1837-1919) at first believed that Liebault was a fake, and set up an investigation to expose him. However, the investigation did not proceed as Bernheim had planned, for while observing Liebault's treatment of his patients he realized that Liebault's hypnotic methods of treatment were having some effect. As a result of his conversion to hypnosis Bernheim started to investigate it scientifically.
He was particularly interested in attempting to understand the phenomenon of hypnotic suggestion, and was able to demonstrate that this suggestion was the main underlying factor in hypnosis. He also showed scientifically that the causes of hypnotic induction were psychological rather than physical. In 1884 he published his book 'De La Suggestion', and two years later he added two chapters dealing with therapeutic approaches using hypnosis, one for hysteria and the other for psychosomatic disorders. Bernheim's contribution to hypnosis is in his demonstration that suggestion is the main factor in hypnosis, and in his rigorous and critical approach to hypnosis and its uses.

JEAN CHARCOT

Jean Martin Charcot (1825-1893) was director of the neurological clinic at the Salpetriere Hospital in Paris. In 1878 when he started to investigate hypnosis he was already a famous and distinguished neurologist. Despite his pre-eminence his investigations gave rise to several false conclusions.

One group of patients that Charcot worked with were suffering from hysteria. He found that hysterical symptoms e.g. paralysis, deafness, blindness, could be induced and removed by hypnosis. He then wrongly assumed that hypnosis and hysteria were closely related, and that furthermore only hysterical persons could be hypnotized. He also believed that hypnosis could be produced by purely physical means, and that it was an organic phenomenon. He put forward a stage theory of hypnosis in which there were three distinct levels of hypnosis, which could be induced and terminated by certain physical stimuli. These stages were lethargy, catalepsy, and somnambulism.

These views were obviously in direct opposition to those of Bernheim and Liebault, and for several years there was much argument between the Nancy School and the Paris group. However, in the end the weight of the evidence produced by the Nancy School convinced Charcot that his views were incorrect.

Charcot's importance lies not in his ideas concerning hypnosis, which were largely erroneous, but in his stature as a doctor and scientist. For him to investigate, use, and write about hypnosis was of great value at a time when it had not yet emerged from the shadow cast by Mesmer. From this point, hypnosis could be accepted much more easily by the medical profession.

PIERRE JANET

Pierre Janet (1859-1947) was one of Charcot's students, and eventually his successor as director of the psychological laboratory at the Salpetriere hospital in Paris. Janet believed that under hypnosis the conscious mind is gradually suppressed, and so the subconscious comes more and more to the fore, and during deep hypnosis it 'takes over' completely. He was particularly interested in trying to explain the theoretical nature of hypnosis.

JOSEPH BREUER

Joseph Breuer (1842-1925) was a colleague of Freud. He suggested that the causes of hysteria were likely to be memories and emotions which were very painful to the subject, and hence were repressed. Under hypnosis the symptoms of hysteria could be removed by asking the patient to talk about these memories and emotions, and relive the experience. Breuer and Freud collaborated on this, and Freud carried on Breuer's work when the latter decided not to carry out any more work in this area.

SIGMUND FREUD

Sigmund Freud (1856-1939) became interested in hypnosis after watching Breuer at work, and in 1885 he went to study with Charcot, and later with Bernheim and Liebault. Freud believed at first that hypnosis could give access to the unconscious, and used it in treating patients with neurotic symptoms. However, as Freud developed his techniques of psychoanalysis, he used hypnosis less and less. There were a number of reasons for this: hypnosis was too time consuming, not all patients could be hypnotized to the same extent, cures were not always permanent, and the patient was too open to suggestions by the therapist and hence there was not enough spontaneity. Freud also found hypnosis difficult to accept as a scientific phenomenon. Since he wanted to investigate the unconscious scientifically; hypnosis, which appeared largely to be based on suggestion and faith, was always likely to be abandoned.
  Whether Freud's abandonment of hypnosis was detrimental or not to the development of hypnosis in the long term is a matter of opinion. On the one hand Freud's reputation was such that when he ceased to use hypnosis, hypnosis experienced a rapid decline in popularity. On the other hand hypnosis was usually used in an authoritarian and stilted manner, and later when its use increased again new and innovative methods were often used, which may not have been so readily developed without this break.

CLARK HULL

Clark L. Hull (1884-1952) represents the increasing interest shown by psychologists in the phenomenon of hypnosis. In 1933 he published his classic book 'Hypnosis and Suggestibility: An Experimental Approach', which because of its rigorous and scientific approach should be read by all those interested in hypnosis. Hull was responsible for setting down a number of questions concerning hypnosis. Fifty years later many of these questions are still unanswered.

MILTON ERICKSON

Milton Erickson (1901-1980) was perhaps responsible for interesting Hull in hypnosis, for in 1923 he gave a graduate seminar on hypnosis at Hull's request. Erickson went on to become probably the most influential, and certainly the most ingenious, hypnotist working in the area of therapy. It is very difficult to describe briefly Erickson's therapy since it is often so personal, but essentially Erickson attempted to enter the patient's world, and carry out the treatment from there. He was not particularly concerned with insight, but set goals for the patient to achieve, often utilizing hypnosis to achieve these goals. Erickson's work will be discussed in detail in a later chapter.

Two important researchers who are still active in the field of hypnosis are Ernest R. Hilgard and Martin T. Orne. Ernest Hilgard has spent most of his professional career at Stanford University where he is now an Emeritus Professor of Psychology. Among his many contributions to the advancement of hypnosis two stand out: his work on hypnosis as a means of relieving pain and his formulation of the theory of neo-dissociation as a means of understanding hypnosis and hypnotic phenomena.

Martin Orne is Director of the Unit for Experimental Psychiatry at the Institute of Pennsylvania Hospital and Professor of Psychiatry at the University of Pennsylvania. Martin Orne has made many contributions to the study of hypnosis, particularly in investigating the differences between simulated and genuine hypnotic behaviour, and in his concern about the forensic uses of hypnosis. The work of these two important scientists will be discussed in more detail in relevant chapters.

Throughout the first half of this century, hypnosis was largely disregarded by the medical authorities. Despite this, much important work was conducted, both in the theoretical and therapeutic context. In 1955 the British Medical Association officially recognized hypnosis as a legitimate therapeutic technique. The American Medical Association followed suit in 1958, as did the American Psychological Association.

PERSONAL REFLECTIONS

Before ending this discussion of the history of hypnosis it is worth noting the contrast between the medical-psychological view of hypnosis and the lay person's view. Whereas the medical-psychological view has developed considerably, the lay view retains a number of misconceptions about hypnosis, which are well documented by Udolf (1981).

These misconceptions can be considered as quite similar to the medical views that pertained in the last half of the nineteenth century. Hence the misconceptions that hypnotists must have dominating personalities, that hypnotized individuals give up control of themselves to the hypnotist, that people always tell the truth under hypnosis, and that a person's normal powers are enhanced under hypnosis. Anyone regularly using hypnosis will recognize these as prominent among the fears and apprehensions that patients have about hypnosis. Unfortunately, from the point of view of changing people's attitudes, the truth is much less dramatic, and as a consequence often less interesting.

SELECTED READING

Gibson, H. B. (1977) <u>Hypnosis</u>, Peter Owen, London
The chapter on the historical background of hypnosis in this book is made very interesting by Gibson's style.

Chapter Two

CURRENT THEORIES OF HYPNOSIS

As we have seen in the last chapter, there has always been a substantial amount of disagreement concerning the nature of hypnosis. This controversy is often considered as hinging on whether or not hypnosis is thought of as some kind of special state, often referred to as a 'trance'. This is an issue which I will return to in the next chapter, but it does need some discussion here to help in understanding the various theories put forward.

The idea that hypnotized subjects are in some kind of special state is one which has arisen for at least two reasons. The first is that hypnotized subjects often report that they feel 'different'. The second is that many writers on hypnosis, particularly earlier ones, have argued that by inducing hypnosis the hypnotist puts the subject into a trance, in which extraordinary feats can be performed, (White, 1941). The vast majority of the evidence gathered since this date and reviewed by Barber (1972) contradicts this. Subjective reports however, are less easily brushed aside, except of course by workers in the behaviourist tradition. Most current workers in the area of hypnosis e.g. Bowers (1976), Hilgard (1975) tend to accept that some subjects are happy to describe their experiences as akin to being in a trance, while accepting that for different subjects these experiences may be different.

As in much of the discussions about hypnosis, it is almost impossible not to be drawn into an argument about the definition of terms. We might expect that hypnotists would have more consensus for the meaning of the term trance than subjects, but a perusal of any two discussions of the term 'trance' by different authors will almost inevitably leave the reader with two different views of the term.

This is perhaps inevitable as the hypnotist's ideas of the meaning of the term are strongly influenced by the reports of his hypnotized subjects, and by his own subjective experiences. Although the concept of the trance in hypnosis is a very interesting one, it has been argued that it is not central to the issue of hypnosis. Hilgard (1975) makes this point very succinctly, arguing that it is the opponents of the concept who are responsible for keeping the issue alive. If we regard the trance as an altered state of consciousness, then in the last resort we are dependent on hypnotized persons' subjective reports, at least until we find an objective way of investigating altered states of consciousness. As we will see, theorists differ in the amount of weight they are prepared to give to subjective reports. In addition many argue that subjects are mistaken in interpreting their experience as a trance state. I believe that this is a crucial issue in hypnosis, and that a theory should aim to explain subjective experiences, rather than reinterpreting them in an attempt to make them fit the particular theory.

I have chosen to discuss seven different theories of hypnosis. Some are well known theories, some are perhaps less well known, but are important because they examine the phenomena of hypnosis from a particular perspective which throws light on the issues involved. I have tried to set down what I believe to be their essential points, but for those readers wishing for a detailed understanding of the theories, the section 'Selected Reading' at the end of the chapter contains a number of references which should provide this.

NEODISSOCIATION THEORY

The chief proponent of this theory is Hilgard (1973a, 1973b, 1974). Neodissociation theory is actually a modification of dissociation theory, which was in vogue at the turn of the century. Hilgard proposes that an individual possesses a number of cognitive systems, which are hierarchically arranged. Hypnosis has the effect of dissociating these systems from one another. Thus a hypnotized subject may report feeling no pain, but the 'hidden observer', which is the name Hilgard gives to the cognitive system which is aware of what is going on, reports feeling pain. According to Hilgard it is possible to make contact with this hidden observer by appropriate instructions given during hypnosis, e.g. 'when I place my hand on your shoulder I will be able to talk to the hidden part of you which is still aware of your body and what it is feeling. When I take my hand off your shoulder the hidden part of you will again be hidden from the part of you I am talking to now'.

Instructions can also be given to enable the subject to talk about what the hidden observer was experiencing during hypnosis, after the hypnotic session has ended. It appears that what is being proposed is that when a subject is hypnotized, only some of his cognitive systems are involved, some remain unaffected. Thus a person who experiences only a vague feeling of relaxation has only a very few low level cognitive systems affected. A person who experiences arm levitation and analgesia has many more cognitive systems affected. It is unclear how many cognitive systems an individual possesses, or even whether it is sensible to ask such a question.

Tart (1970, 1972) has investigated depth of trance by means of a self-report scale which indicates that some subjects may distinguish over twenty depth levels. We might well expect there to be individual differences in the number of cognitive systems people possess, and also differences in the number they are able to differentiate from one another.

It is not clear what the relationship is between trance depth and cognitive systems, although we might expect to find a positive correlation. It seems unlikely that either consists of discrete stages arranged on an interval scale, but rather more likely is that they are arranged on an ordinal scale which differs from individual to individual, and also from time to time.

Hilgard's theory is not incompatible with the idea of hypnosis as an altered state of consciousness, in fact it is quite easy to see how a subject might report that he felt rather unusual if some of his cognitive systems were dissociated from one another. Hilgard (1975) also believes that these systems may be affected by procedures other than hypnotic induction, e.g. fatigue, drugs. The idea of multiple, hierarchically arranged, cognitive control systems is a general theory of cognitive organization, which has relevance in a wide number of areas. The experimental evidence for this theory is, as Wagstaff (1981) concludes, not conclusive. However, it is an important way of conceptualizing hypnotic behaviour, and indeed cognitive organization, and will no doubt stimulate much research and debate.

THE ALTERNATIVE PARADIGM

This rather interesting title for a theory is the one Barber (1979) uses to discuss his approach to hypnosis, in contrast to the special state (trance) paradigm, which he sees as the traditional paradigm. During the last two decades Barber has made clear his dissatisfaction with traditional approaches to hypnosis, generally writing the word 'hypnosis' in quotes to show his dissatisfaction with it. Barber appears to have set himself the goal of identifying the antecedent variables which cause the behaviours identified as occurring during hypnosis. He believes that subjects have positive, task-oriented attitudes, motivations and expectancies, and these allow them to imagine vividly those things which are suggested, simultaneously letting go of extraneous or contrary thoughts.

Barber has made a massive contribution to the sophistication of research design in hypnosis. One of his techniques is to employ what he refers to as 'task motivational instructions'. In this experimental set-up a group of subjects is instructed, very definitely and positively, to act in a particular way. It is clear that this group is under very strong social pressure to obey the instructions given, and indeed Barber and his co-workers often find that using this technique they can apparently duplicate many of the phenomena other researchers produce by using a normal hypnotic induction procedure.

However, it is not clear that subjects actually report what they have experienced. Bowers (1967) argued that the social demands of Barber's experimental technique were such that although some subjects did not experience what they were instructed to experience, they felt obliged to report that they had experienced these things. Also, simply by demonstrating that certain effects can be produced by task motivational instructions does not mean that the same effects cannot be produced another way, e.g. by hypnotic induction procedures. Barber is fully aware of this and argues that until evidence is produced which cannot be explained in any other way than by postulating that subjects are in a hypnotic trance, then it is pointless to invoke the trance explanation when all the phenomena can be explained by high responsiveness to test suggestions (Barber and Ham, 1974).

Bowers has been quite critical of Barber, arguing that:

> no matter how similar the behavioral 'outcome' of hypnosis and task motivation, the latter tends to achieve its effect by coercing overt compliance that does not reflect a person's internal experience but, instead, satisfies the external demands to behave and report in a prescribed manner. Consequently, the behavior of task-motivated subjects does not bear relevantly on a consideration of hypnotic phenomena, which is concerned with suggested (and unsuggested) alterations in 'experience' as they may be revealed in overt behavior and verbal reports (Bowers, 1976, p. 88)

This statement tends to be representative of many made by researchers who hold that hypnosis is a separate, identifiable phenomenon. Barber, although his later work (Wilson and Barber, 1982) seems to indicate a moderation of his attitude, would be unlikely to be convinced.

ROLE ENACTMENT

This theory has been devised and elaborated by Sarbin, although perhaps the best exposition of his standpoint is in Sarbin and Coe (1972). Sarbin approaches hypnosis from the point of view of a social psychologist. He maintains that throughout their lives individuals act out roles which are appropriate to different social situations, and hypnosis is simply one social situation. So just as one might act out the role of 'employee', 'lover', or any one of thousands of roles, so might one act out the role of 'hypnotized person', or for that matter 'hypnotist'.

Both Gibson (1977) and Wagstaff (1981) rightly make the point that this does not mean that the subjects are deliberately faking. They may be genuinely involved with their role in the same way that they are genuinely involved with the other roles in their lives. Due to this involvement, which Sarbin refers to as 'organismic involvement' subjects genuinely believe that they are experiencing the hypnotic behaviour that is suggested to them. When subjects report experiencing hallucinations, Sarbin takes the viewpoint that these are 'believed-in imaginings'; subjects have acted the role of hypnotized persons so well that they actually believe they have experienced the hallucinations.

Although Sarbin has often been considered to have rejected the idea of hypnosis as an altered state of consciousness, this is not so. He considers much of the argument for the trance state to be circular, along the general lines of: these are the characteristic behaviours that subjects show in a trance, this subject is exhibiting these behaviours, therefore the subject must be in a trance. Where Sarbin does not appear to reject the idea that hypnotized subjects are in a different state is in his willingness to accept that subjects' subjective testimony can be an indication that they are in an altered state of consciousness. However, as Sheehan and Perry (1976) point out, Sarbin does not seem happy with the idea of altered states of consciousness and argues that by viewing the phenomena as believed-in imaginings rather than as products of a trance state he is describing the same phenomena more clearly, and in a way which is likely to lead to a better explanation of the situations in which such believed-in imaginings can occur.

PSYCHOANALYTIC THEORY

A number of writers have been instrumental in the development of a psychoanalytic theory of hypnosis including, as one might expect, Freud. As Gruenewald states (1982, p. 185): 'The themes relating to hypnosis which Freud had elaborated in varying degrees were the basis for other psychoanalytic writings on that topic.'

Hilgard (1975) makes the point that the psychoanalytic theory of hypnosis is able to incorporate hypnosis into a much larger theoretical framework, with its own vocabulary and concepts. This makes it very difficult to understand this particular theory of hypnosis without some understanding of psychoanalysis in general. Furthermore the psychoanalytic theory of hypnosis has undergone a number of changes over the past eighty years, the major theoretical stances being charted by Gruenewald (1982).

However, the basic essence of the psychoanalytic viewpoint as expressed by Gill and

19

Brenman (1959) is the interpretation of hypnosis as adaptive regression. Gill and Brenman characterize this regression as being regression in the service of the ego, indicating that the regression is under the control of the ego and can be terminated at will. It is hypothesized that in order to gain increased mastery over inner experiences the ego initiates, controls, and terminates regression, and it does this by temporarily losing contact with reality. Hypnosis is seen as dependent on the affective relationship with the hypnotist, i.e. transference, and is characterized by the ease with which thought processes can be manipulated.

Fromm (1979) has examined various altered states of consciousness, including daydreaming, various relaxation states, states of creativity, the hypnagogic and hypnopompic states, hypnosis, sensory deprivation states, nocturnal dreams, psychedelic states caused by drug use, concentrative and mindful meditation, states of mystical rapture, states of dissociation, states of depersonalization, fugue states and psychotic states, particularly the hallucinatory ones. To help in understanding these states she has used the term 'ego receptivity', which is characterized by a passive taking in of information rather than the normal active processing and manipulation of that information. Her terminology and use of concepts for the explanation of hypnosis is thus psychoanalytically oriented.

It is difficult to come to any clear conclusion about the psychoanalytic stance. It has a very long history, but like much of psychoanalytic theory the basic ideas seem untestable. Very often it appears as if psychoanalytic concepts and words are being used to explain phenomena when in fact they are simply describing the behaviours or experiences of the hypnotized subjects. However, there is no doubt that many psychoanalysts use hypnosis in their work, and interpret it in psychoanalytic terms. Despite this, it is not clear that the psychoanalytic theory of hypnosis is other than a possible description, and as such may be compatible with other explanations, e.g. role enactment theory.

HYPNOSIS AS RELAXATION

Edmonston (1981) has attempted to present an argument that hypnosis and relaxation are essentially extremely similar states. Furthermore, he states that neutral hypnosis is simply the

20

psychobiological condition of relaxation. By neutral hypnosis Edmonston means the state produced in an individual who has just undergone an induction procedure. Edmonston is able to marshal a great deal of evidence to support this view, and in fact the book provides a marvellous source of references in this area.

Obviously one of the problems for Edmonston's theory is that 'alert hypnosis' poses a problem. How can a person who has undergone a hypnotic induction procedure, complied with all the suggested instructions, is then asked to exercise vigorously and does so, be said to be relaxed? Edmonston attempts to counter this criticism by arguing on historical grounds that the 'traditional' view of hypnosis incorporates only 'sleepy-type', relaxation procedures, and alert hypnosis is not really hypnosis in this traditional sense. This is an interesting idea, but not one which I suspect finds much favour with most researchers.

Despite this criticism, many hypnotized people appear to be, and report being, extremely relaxed. However, in a situation in which subjects compared being relaxed using a standard relaxation procedure with hypnotic induction followed by a relaxation procedure, I found that while they reported being physically relaxed in both conditions, they reported cognitive differences. Specifically they reported being mentally alert during the relaxation only session, whereas they felt cognitively 'drowsy' during the relaxation plus induction session. It would seem implicit in Edmonston's theory that there should be no cognitive differences between the two conditions. Edmonston's theory remains an extremely interesting one, and well worth further research.

STRATEGIC ENACTMENT

This is a theory which has been developed by Spanos (1982). He writes (p. 199):

> According to this formulation, hypnotic behavior does not occur automatically, and like other social behavior it can be usefully described as goal-directed action. However, a central demand of the hypnotic situation is that subjects define their responses as involuntary "happenings" rather than self-initiated actions. The experience of involuntariness does not arise because

strategic acts are transformed to automatic ones. Instead, it reflects an interpretation that subjects make about their own behavior.

The point Spanos makes is that much of social behaviour is seen as goal-directed and self-initiated. One of the properties of being hypnotized, however, seems to be that very often actions are perceived as being involuntary. A central component of strategic enactment is the subjects' interpretation of these actions as voluntary.

Spanos identifies a number of components involved in the strategic enactment of 'becoming hypnotized'. Besides the interpretation of certain behaviours as involuntary, these include heightened responsiveness following hypnotic versus nonhypnotic procedures and evidence of possessing a hidden observer. It appears that the ability of individuals to become hypnotized is determined by their ability to strategically enact the behaviours they believe characterize being hypnotized, including subjective experiences. This is clearly not a state theory of hypnosis but is perhaps more akin to role enactment.

According to this theory the knowledge that individuals bring with them to the hypnotic situation and the instructions that they are given by the hypnotist will determine their behaviours and experience during the hypnotic session. If this is the case, then it is difficult to see where spontaneous experiences not part of their previous knowledge, and not suggested by the hypnotist, originate. Furthermore, the theory should predict that when such spontaneous experiences do occur, they should in some sense make the person's experience of hypnosis less genuine.

COMPLIANCE AND BELIEF

Wagstaff (1981) has written an excellent book which details his theoretical approach to hypnosis. He is most definitely a non-state theorist, and interprets hypnotic behaviour in terms of compliance and belief. Compliance is the term used to describe overt behaviour which is like that requested by the hypnotist. However, this overt behaviour does not necessarily reflect the private convictions of the individual. For instance, individuals may act as if they feel no pain, but privately they may be experiencing the pain. Belief is the term used to describe the situation in which private convictions are in accord with public behaviours. If subjects find themselves blinking when told their eyelids are getting heavy, then they may well attribute to themselves the belief that they are becoming hypnotized. Wagstaff argues that private beliefs are just as susceptible to the social demands of the hypnotic situation as external behaviours.

This theory may well be able to account for many of the behaviours shown by some hypnotized individuals. However, as Fellows (1982) concludes in his review of Wagstaff's book, it is not easy to see how the theory can explain individual differences in hypnotic susceptibility. Nor is it clear how the theory incorporates the use of subjective experience as an indication of differing types of hypnotic response.

Despite these criticisms, and the limited range of applicability of the theory, Wagstaff's ideas deserve a wide audience. He has written an excellent book which ranks among the best I have ever read on hypnosis.

PERSONAL REFLECTIONS

What can we conclude from this brief survey of theories of hypnosis? Most importantly, none of them seem to be able to deal adequately with all the phenomena which come under the general heading of hypnosis. This is perhaps not surprising given the tremendous variety of phenomena. Accordingly the theories have different ways of dealing with this variety. Some redefine hypnosis, e.g. Edmonston (1981). Others reinterpret subjective experience, e.g. Spanos (1982). Perhaps the most difficult to evaluate is the psychoanalytic approach, because it requires an acceptance of the basic tenets of psychoanalytic theory.

Despite these inadequacies, each of the theories has something to offer, a new conceptualization of the issues, a methodological approach, a new synthesis of the evidence. Of course, in one sense it is impossible to produce a theory which is satisfactory to all researchers, for they are likely to have different criteria for evaluating theories. Hempel (1966) gives a useful description of the function of theories (p. 70):

Theories are usually introduced when previous study of a class of phenomena has revealed a system of uniformities that can be expressed in the form of empirical laws. Theories then seek to explain those regularities and, generally, to afford a deeper and more accurate understanding of the phenomena in question. To this end, a theory construes those phenomena as manifestations of entities and processes that lie behind or beneath them, as it were. These are assumed to be governed by characteristic theoretical laws, or theoretical principles, by means of which the theory then explains the empirical uniformities that have been previously discovered, and usually also predicts "new" regularities of similar kinds.

The theories I have discussed attempt to fulfil these functions at least partially. The area in which they appear to be not succeeding totally is in explaining all the empirical regularities, particularly those based on personal testimony.

It can be argued that no one theory can ever be sufficient to explain the diverse phenomena of hypnosis. However, I believe this would be a mistake, for it seems to be forcing the evidence to fit the theory rather than revising the theory when it shows itself to be inadequate to cope with the empirical data. Perhaps the greatest stumbling blocks for theories of hypnosis, just as they are for psychology in general, are the individuals' subjective reports. Yet not to incorporate these into the theories is to revert to the view of man as a 'black box'.

Theories of hypnosis need to explain two things. The first is the observed behaviour of hypnotized individuals. In this I include not only typical hypnotic phenomena such as arm levitation, but also physiological correlates, scores on tests of susceptibility (and also scores on other tests if administered within a hypnotic context), and behaviours which occur outside the immediate hypnotic context yet which are related to it, e.g. hypnotically produced amnesia, various therapeutic effects. The second is the subjective experience that hypnotized individuals report. More use should be made of structured interviews, inventories, and particularly protocol analysis, which could well offer a very interesting and useful means of more formally investigating hypnotic experiences (Radford, 1974; Ericsson and Simon, 1980; Byrne, 1983).

It is my guess that in ten years time the

theory of hypnosis which will find most favour is one which incorporates subjective reports while taking account of the demands of the social situation and subjects' expectations. I also suspect that the debate between state and non-state theorists will continue.

SELECTED READING

For those readers who really want to be well informed the books and papers listed below provide a good discussion of theories in hypnosis.

Barber, T. X. (1969) Hypnosis: A Scientific Approach, Van Nostrand, New York
This book is a classic which sets down Barber's original theoretical stance, as well as providing a very useful summary of his own research, which even by 1969 was considerable.

Bowers, K. S. (1976) Hypnosis for the Seriously Curious, Brooks/Cole Publishing Company, Monterey, California
An interesting and well written book organized around a number of questions, which Bowers then attempts to answer. Not exactly bed-time reading, but it does repay time spent on it.

Gruenewald, D. (1982) 'A Psychoanalytic View of Hypnosis', The American Journal of Clinical Hypnosis, 24, 185-190
This is a very interesting review of psychoanalytic theories which certainly provides food for thought.

Wagstaff, G. F. (1981) Hypnosis, Compliance and Belief, The Harvester Press, Brighton
An excellent book. Not only does it contain the exposition of Wagstaff's own theory, it also contains a well-informed discussion of a number of other theories.

Chapter Three

HYPNOSIS AND OTHER STATES OF CONSCIOUSNESS

As should already be apparent, there is considerable disagreement over whether it is necessary to invoke the concept of an 'altered state' in explaining hypnotic phenomena. What I wish to do in this chapter is to attempt to circumvent this argument by proposing that individuals' states of consciousness vary from moment to moment, and that subjective hypnotic experiences represent a variation in this state which individuals may experience as more extreme than their normal range of conscious experiences. In order to do this several areas need to be explored. The first of these is the nature of consciousness.

THE NATURE OF CONSCIOUSNESS

As I sit here in the computer room in the School of Speech Pathology at Leicester Polytechnic writing this book, I am 'conscious' of many things. Foremost is a nagging unease over the phrasing of the first sentence of this paragraph. It seems to convey the meaning I wish it to, but I also believe that it is rather clumsy. For the sake of this explanation of my own conscious awareness, I decide not to revise it, but it still bothers me. I am also aware of attempting internally to 'put into words' the ideas I wish to convey next. In addition to this awareness of what may be termed internal events, I am also aware of external events.
These include the secretary typing in the room across the corridor, the flicker of the monitor screen (I seem more aware of this than the words on the screen), a slight feeling of discomfort in my right leg from sitting in one position too long, and a feeling of being just a little too warm. If I wish

I can choose to direct my attention to any of these external events, to explore them. I can concentrate on the feeling of discomfort in my leg, and as I do so it seems to expand. By this I do not mean that it becomes more severe, rather that it appears to occupy more of my consciousness. Yet at the same time, by thinking about one bodily sensation, I become more aware of other vague discomforts, itches, etc. I note resignedly that I do not appear to be experiencing any pleasurable physical sensations.

This ability to direct attention is a crucial issue in consciousness and hence in hypnosis. As I think about this statement the names of several psychologists enter my conscious awareness. Broadbent is the first of these, followed rapidly by Posner and Schneider. The reason for the appearance of 'Broadbent' seems easy to find; to me Broadbent is closely linked to the concept of attention through his work in this area, e.g. Broadbent (1957). The appearance of 'Posner' and 'Schneider' is rather harder to explain. The reason is, I believe, as follows. Considering the direction of attention lead me to 'think' about situations in which attention could not be directed. This 'reminded' me of automatic and controlled processing, which both Posner and Schneider have written about. I have placed the words 'think' and 'reminded' in single quotation marks because I am sure that neither was a conscious process, but rather examples of automatic processing.

Again I am aware that I feel rather uneasy about the last two names. On looking up what I believe to be the references I was thinking of I find that I was probably slightly mistaken. I am unable to find a dual authored paper by Posner and Schneider, although I still partly believe that if I search longer I may! What I do find is a reference to a paper by Posner and Snyder (1975) and a reference to a paper by Schneider and Shiffrin (1977). I point out for the sake of those who wish to speculate further on this type of confusion the acoustic similarity between 'Schneider' and 'Snyder'.

What conclusions can be drawn from this account of my own subjective experience? First, I am aware of external events; second, I am aware of internal events; third, I appear able to direct my attention in some situations while in others I do not; fourth, I can monitor these shifts of attention; and fifth, and perhaps most difficult to appreciate, I can

27

monitor these awarenesses and explore their quality. This last ability is, I believe, similar to what Oatley (1981, p. 87) has referred to as 'reflective consciousness', and Humphrey (1984, p. 8) as 'reflexive consciousness' or 'consciousness of consciousness'. I am not implying here that there is any hierarchical ordering of these awarenesses, rather they are ways of categorizing the objects of my awareness. Even my monitoring of my awareness is best considered within the same framework, otherwise there seems to be a considerable danger of entering an infinite regress, with layers of awareness, each aware of the one below it. Nor is there any theoretical need to do so; it is more parsimonious simply to assume that monitoring of awareness is not a special case, but is instead merely one of the categories of awareness.

HYPNOSIS AND CONSCIOUSNESS

I hope that the reader who has followed the discussion so far will be beginning to see the importance of this for theories of hypnosis. It is the last category, monitoring of awarenesses, which hypnotized individuals use to make judgements about the depth of their hypnosis, and whether they are in a trance or not. The following example should help to illustrate this.

Janet has undergone an hypnotic induction procedure for the first time. After the session is over she talks about her experience.

I felt very relaxed, not just my body, but my mind, somehow. Not sleepy, but rather as if I was letting my attention wander wherever it wished. When you asked me to think of something very pleasant which had happened to me when I was younger, I found it quite difficult to concentrate on any one thing. The arm levitation was a surprise. I was thinking to myself 'I can't do this' when my arm started to rise. It definitely happened on its own. I was a bit worried at first because I wasn't sure if I could control it. I didn't make any effort to force it down, but I felt as if I might not have been able to if I had tried. I soon stopped worrying and just concentrated on feeling what was happening. I could picture the seashore really well when you suggested it, I

didn't want to leave. I didn't want to wake up
either, you could have made it last longer. I
enjoyed it. I felt different, but it was a nice
feeling.

If we examine this report in detail we can see the
categories of objects of Janet's awareness
encapsulated within this report. Awareness of
external events is clearly present, as indicated by
Janet's perception of my voice. Janet is also aware
of internal events, since she says she was slightly
worried at one point. She is certainly monitoring
her attentional shifts, as she is able to report
that she feels her attention is wandering rather
than being directed. When Janet says she felt
different, it is, I believe, as a result of
monitoring her own awarenesses.

During the hypnotic session Janet was aware of
different experiences. When she reflects on those
experiences she comes to the conclusion that she
felt different. There are several reasons for this
conclusion. One is that she believes her attention
to be wandering. She finds her ability to picture
the seashore impressive. Most compelling of all is
that her arm starts to move under its own volition.
More than that even, Janet is thinking that it is
not going to move when it suddenly starts to do so.
She experiences a certain amount of disparity
between her awareness of external and internal
events. She is not aware of giving her arm a command
to move, but she is also aware that it is moving.
These reasons lead her to believe that she felt
different.

But would this also lead Janet to believe she
was in a trance? This of course depends on what she
believes a trance to be. If Janet's view of a trance
is as a situation in which she feels different, the
answer is yes. If her view of a trance is as a
situation in which she totally loses touch with
reality, then the answer is no. Clearly there will
be large individual differences in this respect. But
these problems can be circumvented by asking Janet
how different from normal she feels under hypnosis,
for Janet is the best judge of her conscious
experiences.

More information can be obtained about these
differences in a variety of ways, by using
structured interviews, protocol analysis and self-
report scales of depth (Tart, 1979). Tart reports
that he is very impressed with the Extended North
Carolina Scale and believes it to be the most useful

measure of hypnotic depth he has seen. It is an open ended scale, with no limit to its depth, so if subjects felt they were hypnotized deeply enough they could report a depth of one hundred, or even one thousand. As Tart points out scales of depth can be used in non-hypnotic contexts, e.g. drug induced states, meditation, and of course under ordinary conditions (although we would not expect much 'depth' to be reported here). The Extended North Carolina Scale consists of a series of numbers with defined values at particular points on the scale. These are:

0	=	waking
1-12	=	relaxed,detached, ideomotor movements
20	=	analgesia
25	=	dreams
30	=	amnesia, mental quiet, very high suggestibility
40	=	all effects completely real
50+	=	mind sluggish

As I mentioned at the beginning of this chapter, I believe that individuals' states of consciousness vary from one moment to the next. Using a depth scale like the one above tends to bear this out, for while the scale is not really sensitive enough to pick out many differences in depth under normal conditions, it is possible to demonstrate that there are some individually reliable differences. To assume that consciousness cannot vary from moment to moment is to deny our own experiences. When we monitor our awarenesses we make conclusions about the general condition or state of our consciousness. Unfortunately, most individuals do not have a very good vocabulary for conveying information about these states, and it is only when their present state changes quite dramatically they find the words to talk about it.

This seems an appropriate point at which to sum up the views presented so far. I am arguing that we judge our state of consciousness as a result of monitoring our awarenesses, and this is the case whether we are hypnotized or not. Our state of consciousness varies from moment to moment, but under normal conditions this is not a dramatic variation. Under hypnosis however, some individuals may experience a considerable difference from normal when they monitor their awarenesses, and this may lead them to say their state of consciousness is quite different.

In much of the argument about whether or not hypnosis is an altered state of consciousness the wide variety of states (Ludwig, 1969) often seems to be overlooked. This is a pity for it has given rise to the belief that when researchers speak of hypnosis as an altered state of consciousness what they are implying is that hypnosis is one state of consciousness, normal functioning is another, meditation is another, etc.

Perhaps this fallacy can be exposed by a close examination of an hypnotic session. Janet can again serve as our example. Before the hypnotic induction procedure Janet is normally alert, and on monitoring her awarenesses characterizes them as normal. During suggestions of eye closure she perceives her state as being slightly less alert. Here is the first reported change of state, probably brought about by her awareness that her eyelids are flickering, she feels physically comfortable and quite relaxed. Her awareness that her attention is wandering reinforces her belief that she is not as alert as previously; it may even be sufficient to lead her to report that her state has changed yet again, becoming definitely less alert than previously. Her awareness that her arm is rising when she did not expect it to, and her awareness that she is worried are likely to lead to her reporting another change of state, but not necessarily one in which she is less alert still. One way in which this can be resolved is to conclude that she is in a different state in which it is accepted that these kind of things can happen, so she reports simply that she feels different, for she has no words adequately to describe her state of consciousness.

It is not my contention that for hypnotic phenomena to occur, e.g. arm levitation, analgesia, hallucinations etc., individuals must first enter a different state of consciousness, rather, individuals make judgements about their state of consciousness based on their awareness of the phenomena they are experiencing. However, once a person realizes their state of consciousness is different from normal, this may make it easier for other typical hypnotic phenomena to occur. If we once again consider Janet's experiences, this should become clear.

What happens to Janet is that once she experiences one phenomenon, relaxation, she monitors her awareness of events, and decides that her state of consciousness is different. By perceiving her state of consciousness to be different, I believe

31

that it is more likely she will experience other hypnotic phenomena, because she expects that being in a different state may well lead to different experiences. If she consequently experiences more hypnotic phenomena, this will again lead to a perceived change of state, which again will make the experience of hypnotic events more likely, and so the circle continues. But obviously this circle is not unending. At some stage in this process Janet may well decide that her state of consciousness is sufficiently different for all the hypnotic phenomena suggested to occur. Or she may not experience one or more of the suggested phenomena, which may bring her state of consciousness closer to normal. Clearly individual differences would also be expected here, which would account for at least some of the individual differences in susceptibility.

Jaynes (1976) has noted the prevalence in Western Civilization of the 'container' metaphor to characterize the mind. Thus we speak of open minds, closed minds, shallow minds, of having ideas deep in our minds, of having deep corners in our minds where ideas lurk, and a whole host of other spatial metaphors. This metaphor has also probably been responsible for the consideration of hypnosis as having a variety of 'depths'. However, metaphors have their limitations, and often constrain the ways in which we construe events. I should like to sketch out another metaphor, which is concerned primarily with our awareness of events, and how hypnosis may affect this.

In this metaphor I want you to imagine a large television screen, with a number of meters beside it. On this screen are a large number of what appear to be separate images. Some of these are larger than others. This screen has a peculiar property. If you stare at one image it appears to expand, while the others get smaller, although they do not totally disappear. If you then look at another image, the former begins to shrink, while this one starts to expand. Sometimes you are drawn to one image without any conscious effort. Every so often you also look at the meters beside the screen. These all seem to be concerned with the quality of the images, how well the apparatus is functioning and, surprisingly, whether or not you are consciously directing your vision.

This is of course a metaphorical explanation of awareness of events and direction of attention. It is an extremely simple one, and its sole purpose is to demonstrate the possible ways in which hypnosis may affect these processes. One possibility is that hypnosis may alter the size of images on the screen irrespective of whether you are looking at them or not. This would be equivalent to a difference in the magnitude of the stimulus, brought about by hypnotic suggestion and having its effect before direction of attention takes place. The work of Hilgard and Hilgard (1983) on hypnosis and pain imply that this is unlikely.

Another possibility is that hypnosis may alter your ability to direct your attention. So it always seems to be either directed to specified images without any conscious control or to be aimlessly scanning over some or all of the images. A third possibility is that the expansion of the image when you are looking at it may be affected by hypnosis. Perhaps the rate of expansion may be increased or decreased, there may be no expansion at all, or there may even be a reduction in size. This would be hypnosis working after direction (or nondirection!) of attention had occurred.

Hypnosis may also affect the meters which monitor how well everything is operating. Here hypnosis would be altering your monitoring of awarenesses. If these are altered, then I would hypothesize that you would report an altered state of consciousness. While the metaphor remains only a metaphor, as more evidence becomes available it should become clearer at what stages hypnosis is operating, but for the moment I hope the reader finds these speculations both interesting and thought provoking.

Part of the purpose of this chapter is to compare hypnosis with other phenomena with which it has been traditionally closely linked. The ones I have chosen are sleep, relaxation, meditation, and drug-induced states.

HYPNOSIS AND SLEEP

Although all of us sleep, we obviously cannot gain a great knowledge of sleep from our own experiences. It is the advent of scientific research in this area, particularly the development of the electroencephalogram (EEG), which has dramatically increased our knowledge of sleep and dreams. To obtain an EEG, electrodes are attached to the scalp to measure changes in the electrical activity of the brain. Dement and Kleitman (1957) identified four distinct stages of sleep using EEG recordings.

During Stage 1 the trace on the EEG recording is of waves of high frequency and low amplitude, much as in the waking resting state (Stage 0), but more irregular. Here the individual is drowsing, and may even deny having been asleep if awakened at this stage.

Stage 2 is characterized by larger and slower waves, which have occasional short runs of rhythmic low frequency waves, called spindles. Stage 2 sleep is deeper than Stage 1 sleep. Deeper still is Stage 3 sleep. Here the trace is of waves that are still irregular and possess spindles, but are of greater amplitude. There may also be occasional, large slow waves. Stage 4 is the deepest of all and is characterized by large slow (delta) waves. The other stage of sleep is REM (Rapid Eye Movement) sleep, in which dreaming occurs. During a night of sleep, individuals, on average, experience five distinct periods of REM sleep at about ninety minute intervals, and they pass between the various stages during the course of the night.

When EEG recordings are taken from hypnotized individuals there appear to be considerable differences from recordings of sleep Stage 2, 3, and 4 (Evans, 1982), e.g. there is little evidence of Stage 4 delta waves occurring during hypnosis. Chertok and Kramarz (1959) discuss EEG similarities between Stage 1 sleep and hypnosis. This could of course be due in part to hypnotic suggestions that the subject feels sleepy, is closing his eyes and perhaps even sleeps for a second or two. Or, as Evans (1979, 1982) points out, it could be due to the insensitivity of EEG recordings. There may be differences in the electrical activity of the brain, but the EEG recordings have so much noise that these are masked. As might be expected, EEG recordings appear quite different when 'alert' induction techniques are carried out as opposed to 'sleepy' ones (Banyai, Meszaros and Greguss, 1981).

It is easy to see why hypnosis was once equated with sleep. To the observer the sleeping individual and the person hypnotized by a 'sleepy' procedure look quite similar. Apparently involuntary movements may occur in both, as may vivid dreams. Another possible area of similarity is in the finding (Evans, 1977) that subjects' scores on the Harvard Group Scale of Hypnotic Susceptibility: Form A, correlated with a question about their ability to fall asleep at night. Evans (1982) has proposed that this could be due to a mechanism which has control over the level of functioning or conscious state, and is involved when the individual enters either hypnosis or sleep. Despite these similarities, sleep and hypnosis are generally thought of as quite different.

HYPNOSIS AND RELAXATION

There can be no doubt that often a hypnotized subject looks very similar to one who is relaxed, whether this relaxation has occurred as a result of an induction procedure by another individual or not. Yet there can also be no doubt that to argue that two phenomena are the same just because they look similar is an error. To investigate the relationship between hypnosis and relaxation it is necessary to investigate much more than just the 'appearance' of the subject.

As mentioned in the previous chapter Edmonston (1981) has argued for the similarity of hypnosis and relaxation states, and I do not intend to reiterate here his thesis or the arguments against it. Rather I should like to examine the reasons why hypnosis and relaxation are often considered to be so similar. The first reason is that hypnotic induction techniques often involve relaxation procedures. For instance, the progressive relaxation method of hypnotic induction involves relaxing each muscle group in turn until the whole body is relaxed. This may also make use of Jacobson's technique (1938) in which each set of muscles is tensed before it is relaxed. It is not surprising that if subjects are given instructions to relax they appear to follow them.

Another reason, as Wagstaff (1981) has pointed out, is that very often when subjects ask what it is like to be hypnotized, they are told it feels like being relaxed. It is to be expected that many subjects will interpret their feelings as a state of relaxation when their expectations are established in this way.

Edmonston (1981) reviews much of the physiological data from the states of relaxation and hypnosis, including EEG, blood chemistry, blood pressure, heart rate, peripheral blood flow, respiration, metabolism, body temperature and electrodermal measures. He concludes that there are no real differences in measures from the two states. Whether this reflects a genuine similarity in the physiological measures underlying each state or merely the bluntness of the measuring instruments is arguable.

In conclusion, I do not believe that relaxation is a necessary concomitant of hypnosis, for it is rather absurd to argue that an individual who is exercising vigorously or experiencing an abreaction is relaxed. Rather I believe it more sensible to hold that if the hypnotic induction procedure includes suggestions of relaxation, and/or if the subject expects to feel relaxed, it is hardly surprising if the subject looks relaxed, reports feeling relaxed, and has the physiological signs of a relaxed person. Surely no other explanation is needed.

MEDITATION

Meditation has often been associated with religion (Maupin, 1969), as a means of attuning oneself with God, a higher being, nature, or everything. It has often been thought of as an altered state of consciousness, in which one may experience insights and revelations, which although they appear very profound at the time are often difficult to appreciate after the period of meditation has ended. In this state, also often referred to as a trance, the experienced meditator will be relaxed and may also be impervious to pain. One method of meditation made popular by the Maharishi Mahesh Yogi is called 'transcendental meditation' or TM, which involves repeating a word or sound called a 'mantra' until the person has reached the desired depth of trance.

Benson and Klipper (1976) and Benson, Kotch, Crassweller and Greenwood (1977) have outlined some general principles which if followed are likely to result in an experience very similar to meditation. The person should sit with eyes closed, and slowly relax each muscle group in turn, beginning with the feet and progressing upwards. Breathing should be nasal and rhythmic, while the subject repeats a word. This should preferably take place in a quiet environment, but it is not necessary for there to be any mystical accompaniments.

From this description there appear similarities in the meditation techniques to self-hypnosis, and certainly some of the phenomena of meditation, e.g. relaxation and analgesia, may also be experienced under hypnosis. However, hypnosis appears to be a broader concept than meditation, and meditation is perhaps usefully considered as a type of hypnosis.

DRUG-INDUCED STATES

Drugs have been used for many thousands of years to produce altered states of consciousness, and although the definitions of an altered state of consciousness are no clearer there is less controversy surrounding the idea that drugs may produce an altered state of consciousness. Despite this, the effects of drugs vary according to the drug-taker's expectations and surroundings, as well as dosage and various other factors, and it is the subject's reports (and perhaps observers' clinical observations) which gives rise to the belief that drugs may produce an altered state of consciousness. To examine the similarities between hypnosis and drug induced states I will discuss the effects of three classes of drugs. These are depressants, stimulants and hallucinogens.

Depressants include one of the most popular of all drugs, alcohol. At relatively low blood alcohol concentrations (0.05 per cent) alertness is reduced, judgement impaired and inhibition lessened. As concentrations increase reaction times lengthen, motor performance becomes more and more impaired, and perceptions are increasingly faulty. At a concentration of 0.35 per cent surgical anaesthesia will occur, and possibly death. Barbiturates are depressants which may be prescribed as relaxants for individuals under stress, or as sleeping pills. Increasing the intake of barbiturates has roughly the same effect as increasing the intake of alcohol. Opiates do not affect sensory and motor performance in the same way as other depressants.

The class of stimulants include two of the most common of all drugs, caffeine and nicotine. Caffeine is usually taken into the body in coffee or tea, whereas nicotine is present in tobacco, which is usually smoked, although it is sometimes chewed. Interestingly, nicotine may be a relaxant rather than a stimulant given particular surroundings and expectations on the part of the user. Another group of stronger stimulants is the amphetamines, of which the pills known as Dexedrine and Benzedrine are currently the most popular. They increase alertness and reduce fatigue by increasing activity in the central nervous system. Another popular drug is cocaine, which like amphetamines increases alertness, and lets the user work and think longer without fatigue.

Hallucinogens typically produce distortions of perception. Marijuana is the best known of these.

Another well known hallucinogen is lysergic acid diethylamide (LSD). The latter was particularly in demand a few years ago for 'expanding consciousness'. The effects of these drugs again vary according to the surroundings and expectations of the users. In some circumstances LSD may produce very frightening experiences.

After this brief survey it should be becoming clear where the similarities may lie between the effects of drugs and hypnosis. The first point to stress is the comparative safety of hypnosis. Some of the drugs mentioned above are generally considered safe, e.g. caffeine, whereas others, e.g. heroin are considered highly dangerous. Hypnosis, of course, is not a drug. Certainly some of the effects of drugs such as analgesia, relaxation and arguably hallucinations, can occur under hypnosis. However, the hypnotized person generally feels much more in control of events, although it could be argued that under the influence of drugs the experiences seem more real. Perhaps the greatest similarity between hypnosis and drugs is that their effects vary according to the surroundings and expectations of the persons involved. There seems little doubt that drugs produce a physiological effect on the central nervous system, but the interpretation of that effect varies from individual to individual, just as the effect of hypnosis varies according to the circumstance.

PERSONAL REFLECTIONS

Despite some excellent work and literature in this area e.g. Tart (1969), Tart (1979), much remains unclear. The relationship between hypnosis and other states of consciousness, while interesting in many respects, is, I believe, far less valuable than understanding the relationship between hypnosis and consciousness in general. The recent upturn in interest in consciousness as an area of study, e.g. Underwood and Stevens (1979, 1981), is to be greatly applauded. As knowledge of consciousness increases, so the integration of hypnosis within a general framework of consciousness becomes more and more likely. But not yet.

SELECTED READING

Fromm, E. and Shor, R. E. (1979) (eds.) <u>Hypnosis:</u>

38

Developments in Research and New Perspectives,
Aldine Publishing Company, New York
This excellent handbook contains several interesting
chapters in areas relevant to the discussions here,
including one by Tart on measuring trance depth.

Tart, C. T. (1969) Altered States of Consciousness,
John Wiley and Sons, Inc., New York
Although it will soon be twenty years old this book
presents a tremendous introduction to the topics
covered in this chapter, with masses of useful
background material.

Underwood, G. and Stevens, R. (1979) (eds.) Aspects
of Consciousness: vol. 1, Psychological Issues,
Academic Press, London
and
Underwood, G. and Stevens, R. (1979) (eds.) Aspects
of Consciousness: vol. 2 , Structural Issues,
Academic Press, London
Both these books contain highly interesting chapters
on various aspects of consciousness, and are really
essential reading for those interested in the issue
of consciousness.

Chapter Four

HYPNOTIZABILITY

Hypnotizability refers to the ease with which a person can be hypnotized. Irrespective of one's theoretical stance concerning the nature of hypnosis it is interesting to consider to what extent hypnotizability is a stable personality trait and to what extent it depends on situational variables. Some writers, e.g. Udolf (1981), have used the term hypnotic susceptibility to refer to the stable personality trait aspect of hypnotizability. Many writers, e.g. Frischholz, Spiegel, Spiegel, Balma and Markell (1982) use the term hypnotic responsivity, which appears to cover both personality and situational variables, while Gibson (1983) argues that responsivity is best used to refer to subjects' responses on particular occasions.

Quite clearly this varying use of different terms can give rise to some confusion. In this discussion I will follow Udolf's definitions (1981, p. 323):

Hypnotizability - the ability of a subject to be hypnotized. Takes into account both basic hypnotic susceptibility and transient motivational factors.
Hypnotic Susceptibility - a personality characteristic of a subject which determines his ability to be hypnotized and to attain a given depth of trance.

Hypnotic responsivity I shall use to refer to subjects' degree of response on particular occasions. However, in practice the boundaries between these different aspects become very fuzzy, and it is often totally impossible to separate them in real situations. This matter will be re-examined when treatment responsivity is discussed in a later chapter.

The problem then arises of how to measure these variables. This is a problem which is very familiar to psychologists, for very few personality traits manifest themselves in the same fashion and in the same degree irrespective of the situation (Mischel, 1968). The approach taken to the solution of this problem has been the construction of standardized tests. Each test is administered as far as possible in the same manner each time it is used to minimize situational variables, so in this sense it is aiming to measure hypnotic susceptibility. However, clearly the motivational state of the subjects cannot be totally controlled, so at the same time it is also measuring hypnotizability.

If hypnotic susceptibility tests were measuring only susceptibility, little or no variation would be expected when the subjects were retested, providing that hypnotic susceptibility is a relatively stable characteristic. If this is the case, then a group of subjects might be expected to maintain their same relative positions if retested on the same test and even if tested on another test of hypnotic susceptibility. Subjects who got a high score would be expected to continue to score high, subjects with a mid-range score would be expected to get a mid-range score on future occasions, and subjects who were low in susceptibility would be expected to remain low.

Bowers (1976) quotes test-retest correlation coefficients as ranging from 0.8 to 0.9. Taking the lower figure of the range this means that the stable personality trait of hypnotic susceptibility, which is what the test is purporting to measure, is accounting for 0.64 of the variance, or in other words 0.36, or over a third, of the variance is accounted for by other variables. It seems fairly safe to assume that these variables are situational in nature. However, this should not be taken as meaning that for any individual their hypnotizability will be two thirds due to their personality trait of hypnotic susceptibility and one third due to situational variables. For instance, it is to be expected that some individuals will respond much more to situational variation than others, as has been demonstrated in experiments in a wide variety of contexts.

INFORMAL TESTS

In addition to the use of standardized tests, there are also more informal tests which can be carried out. These are informal tests which usually require the subject to produce an ideomotor response to suggestions by merely imagining performing the action, rather than actually performing it. Eysenck and Furneaux (1945) have labelled them tests of primary suggestibility. They have also found significant positive correlations between these tests and tests of hypnotic susceptibility.

These informal tests are therefore quite useful, particularly to the clinician. In addition they provide clients with useful experience of what it feels like to experience something without apparent conscious volition, prior to the hypnotic session itself. A number of these informal tests are outlined below. Note that there are many minor variations possible in the procedures for carrying out these tests, in contrast to the standardized tests, the results of which are likely to be invalid if the detailed procedures are not followed exactly.

Body Sway

This is a test which is best carried out individually, for the tester needs to be able to prevent the subject from falling over if a dramatic response is shown. The instructions I usually employ for this informal test are given below. Imagine that the subject has just stepped forward.

'Please stand facing me with the chair behind you. If you find your shoes difficult to balance in, please take them off. I am going to suggest that you can feel a breeze blowing on your back, and gradually this breeze will get stronger and stronger. As you imagine the breeze getting stronger and stronger you imagine yourself leaning forward. In fact even though you have not made any conscious decision to lean forward, you may find yourself actually falling forward. Don't worry, I will catch you. If you fall backwards instead the chair is there to catch you. Alright? Now close your eyes. Just imagine a breeze blowing gently on your back, blowing your hair forward a little. As you imagine your hair being blown forward the breeze seems to be getting stronger and stronger. It definitely feels stronger and stronger, and you can imagine it pushing you forwards. It is getting stronger all the time, pushing you forwards, getting stronger and stronger.'

This can be continued for a reasonable length of time until the tester is satisfied. I usually find two minutes quite adequate, believing that if subjects have shown little body sway by then, the only reason they will show more is fatigue. It is also valuable to know that some subjects occasionally fall forward almost as soon as they have shut their eyes, so be prepared to catch them.

The Chevreul Pendulum

Next to swinging a gold watch and the 'Touch of God' induction procedure, this is about the most impressive piece of apparatus used in hypnosis from the point of view of the ordinary person. It consists of a glass sphere or pyramid on a chain, which is held by the subject like a pendulum. Of course, any suitable pendulum would suffice, but it is hard to resist the temptation of a cut-glass sphere!

In this test subjects are asked to hold the pendulum in one hand and to imagine the pendulum moving in a particular direction, perhaps from side to side, or in a circle. The subjects' eyes may be open or closed, the subject may be seated or not, perhaps with their elbows supported. This is a very good test to carry out as a demonstration, for as Udolf (1981) reports, most subjects are able to perform it with the greatest of ease. It does mean however that many individuals pass it who are not particularly susceptible to hypnosis.

The Headfall Test

This is a very simple test in which if individuals are susceptible to hypnosis, their heads fall forward. The subjects are generally seated, looking straight ahead, with their eyes open. They are then told to close their eyes, and are asked to imagine their heads getting heavier and heavier and gradually falling forward. From informal observation I have noted that this test seems to discriminate quite well between individuals, some members of the group generally having their heads resting on their chests, while others do not appear to have moved their heads at all.

Arm Levitation

This is an impressive test in which the subjects sit or stand with both arms stretched out in front of them. They are then asked to imagine that one hand is getting lighter than the other. If the tester wishes some reason can be suggested for this, e.g. it is being drawn up by a special magnet. After a short time susceptible subjects should have this hand considerably higher than the other. Subjects usually find this a convincing demonstration, if it is effective for them.

Arm Heaviness

This can be considered as the reverse of the above, except that subjects, after assuming a position with their arms outstretched, are asked to imagine one hand getting heavier and heavier, perhaps as a result of something resting on it. In susceptible subjects this arm should gradually lower, but perhaps a more commendable feat is keeping the other arm parallel against the pull of gravity! This is clearly not such an impressive test as arm levitation.

Odour Test

In this test the experimenter uncorks a bottle and asks subjects to raise their hands as soon as they smell the contents of the bottle. The bottle in fact contains nothing but water. This is quite an interesting test, which is really aiming to produce an olfactory hallucination.

Hand Attraction

In this test subjects are asked to put their hands a few inches apart, with the palms facing each other. They are then asked to imagine their hands being pulled together. In some variations of this the subjects are asked to imagine that they are holding a magnet in each hand, and this will cause their hands to be attracted to one another.

Hand Repulsion

This is the opposite of the above test, subjects being asked to imagine that their hands are repelling one another.

44

Hand Clasping
This particular test appears very popular among stage hypnotists. Subjects are asked to extend their arms in front of them, with their palms facing away from them. They are then asked to interlock their fingers, and push outwards. They are then told that their fingers are stuck tightly together, and that when they try to separate their hands they will be unable to. Indeed when they are asked to try many will find it extremely difficult. If readers try this for themselves they will find that it is actually quite difficult to separate their hands. What is required is to relax the hands slightly rather than continuing to push outwards. The tester can note the amount of effort required by subjects to separate their hands, if in fact they are successful at all.

It is important to be clear on the reason for giving these type of tests. If the purpose is to provide a quick guide to hypnotizability then clearly the test selected should be one which discriminates well between individuals, and can also be graded by the tester, perhaps on a one to five scale. For instance in the headfall test the amount of headfall can be observed and graded quite easily for a particular subject. However, if the purpose of the test is to demonstrate susceptibility to a group or to give individuals the belief that they will be good subjects, then a test which is very easy to pass should be selected.

Before moving on to examine standardized tests in detail, it is well worth discussing the explanation of ideomotor suggestion proposed by Hull (1933). Hull argued that normally when individuals imagine certain actions they have a tendency to perform those actions, albeit it to much lesser extent than if they were consciously producing the action. He believed that when individuals did not respond to these type of ideomotor tests that it was due either to the physical response being inhibited, or to failure to imagine the action. The point to note is that Hull is stating that individuals would normally be expected to make some response to the suggestions. As Wagstaff (1981) concludes, if Hull is correct, then these sort of tests would be expected to be excellent at selecting those individuals who are poor hypnotic subjects. However, a recent experimental study by Spanos, Weekes and de Groh (1984) does not support the ideomotor hypothesis.

STANDARDIZED TESTS

The principles relating to the construction of standardized tests are probably well known to the reader, but for anyone who wishes to know more about this area, then the text by Anastasi (1982) provides an excellent introduction. Tests of hypnotic susceptibility generally take the following form. Subjects are given a standard induction procedure, and are then given suggestions to carry out. Some of these suggestions are relatively easy, others are much more difficult. Subjects can be given a score of hypnotic susceptibility based on how many suggestions they carry out.

Barber Suggestibility Scale (BSS)
This scale was developed by Barber (1965). In line with Barber's general views concerning hypnosis, he uses the term 'suggestibility' rather than 'susceptibility'. The scale can be administered with or without an induction procedure. It consists of eight items. These are:

1. Arm lowering
2. Arm levitation
3. Hand lock
4. 'Thirst' hallucination
5. Verbal inhibition
6. Body immobility
7. 'Post-hypnotic-like' response, coughing
8. Selective amnesia

The scoring of these items is strictly defined in the test procedures, and there is both an objective and a subjective score. In the objective scoring scale the subject gets a score of one for each item if the response is according to the criteria given, except that half-point scores are possible for items 3, 4, 5 and 6. To obtain the subjective score the tester asks the subjects whether they actually experienced the suggested effect, or whether they merely went along with the suggestions to please the tester. If the subjects affirm that they actually experienced a suggestion, they are given a score of one for that particular item. (An alternative method is to use a three-point scale). There is no need to question them about items for which they got an objective score of zero; this gets zero automatically on the subjective scoring scale.

Two of the items are 'direct motor' suggestions
(1 and 2), three are 'motor challenge' items (3, 5
and 6), while the other three are 'cognitive'
suggestions (4, 7 and 8), (Fellows, 1979). The test
takes about twenty minutes to carry out, and is
quite straightforward to administer and score. Test-
retest correlations range from 0.80 to 0.88.

Children's Hypnotic Susceptibility Scale (CHSS)
This was devised by London (1963). It has two forms:
one for children from five to thirteen years of age,
and one for adolescents from thirteen to seventeen.
There are in fact no differences in the items on the
two forms, but the instructions and procedures
differ to take account of the different age-related
abilities of the two groups of children. The scale
is in two parts. The first part contains the
following items:

1. Postural sway
2. Eye closure
3. Hand lowering
4. Arm immobilization
5. Finger lock
6. Arm rigidity
7. Hands moving together
8. Verbal inhibition (name)
9. Auditory hallucination (fly buzzing)
10. Eye catalepsy
11. Post-hypnotic suggestion (standing up)
12. Amnesia

The second part contains the following items:

13. Reinduction by post-hypnotic signal
14. Visual and auditory television
    hallucination
15. Cold hallucination
16. Anaesthesia
17. Taste hallucination
18. Smell hallucination
19. Visual hallucination (rabbit)
20. Age regression
21. Dream induction
22. Awakening and post-hypnotic suggestion

These items can each be scored objectively either on
a four point scale or on a dichotomous scale,
depending on the tester. Obviously these two scoring

methods cannot be used interchangeably when scoring
a single person. There is also a subjective
involvement score, using a three point scale, which
is designed to distinguish between 'true' responses
and role-playing. Test-retest reliability is
typically about 0.92.

Creative Imagination Scale
This was developed by Wilson (Wilson and Barber,
1978), and although it is labelled as a test of
creative imagination it contains standard hypnotic-
like suggestions. It contains the following items:

1. Arm heaviness
2. Hand levitation
3. Finger anaesthesia
4. Water 'hallucination'
5. Olfactory-gustatory 'hallucination'
6. Music 'hallucination'
7. Temperature 'hallucination'
8. Time distortion
9. Age regression
10. Mind-body relaxation

This is a self-scoring test in which the subjects
are required to rate their ability to imagine each
item on a five point scale. According to Udolf
(1981) the CIS has a split-half reliability of 0.89,
and a correlation of 0.6 with the BSS. Hilgard,
Sheehan, Monteiro and Macdonald (1981) report a
correlation of 0.55 with the Harvard Scale. The CIS
can be used without an induction procedure, and is
phrased in a non-authoritarian manner.

Harvard Group Scale of Hypnotic Susceptibility
(HGSHS)
This was developed by Shor and Orne (1962) for group
work. It is derived from form A of the Stanford
Hypnotic Susceptibility Scale, and contains the
following items:

1. Head falling
2. Eye closure
3. Hand lowering (left hand)
4. Arm immobilization (right arm)
5. Finger lock
6. Arm rigidity (left)
7. Moving hands together
8. Communication inhibition

9. Experiencing of a fly
10. Eye catalepsy
11. Post-hypnotic suggestion (touching left ankle)
12. Amnesia (depends on number of items recalled)

The test takes about an hour to complete, and is self-scored.

Group Alert Trance Scale (GAT)
This is an interesting although little referred to test devised by Vingoe (1968a, 1968b). As opposed to the more traditional 'sleepy-type' induction procedures used by other tests, this one uses an 'alert-type' induction procedure, in which suggestions are made in parallel for both body relaxation and mind alertness. It contains the following items:

1. Head falling
2. Alert trance
3. Communication inhibition
4. Post-hypnotic suggestion
5. Post-hypnotic amnesia

Each item is self-scored on a four point scale, and the test takes about forty-five minutes in all. Vingoe (1973) reports that it has a correlation of 0.64 with the Harvard Group Scale of Hypnotic Susceptibility, Form A.

Hypnotic Induction Profile (HIP)
This test was developed by Spiegel (1976, 1977), Spiegel and Spiegel (1978) and Stern, Spiegel and Nee (1979) for clinical use, and is designed to be administered individually. The hypnotic induction procedure makes no mention of the words hypnosis, trance or sleep, so it would be suitable in situations where it was thought advisable not to use these terms. It contains six items:

1. Eye roll
2. Dissociation
3. Arm levitation
4. Control differential
5. Cut-off
6. Float

These items are administered on a five point scale.

49

The test can be administered very quickly. Test-retest reliability is about 0.76. Frischholz, Tryon, Vellios, Fisher, Maruffi and Spiegel (1980) have obtained a correlation of 0.63 between the Hypnotic Induction Profile and the Stanford Hypnotic Susceptibility Scale, Form C. However, there is considerable debate as to which items on the profile are positively related to hypnotizability (Hilgard, 1981a, Frischholz, Spiegel, Tryon and Fisher, 1981, and Hilgard, 1981b).

Stanford Hypnotic Clinical Scale for Children
This scale was devised by Morgan and Hilgard (1979), and contains two forms, one for children aged between four and eight years, the other for children aged between 6 and 16 years. The form for younger children contains the following six items:

1. Hand lowering
2. Arm rigidity
3. TV - visual
4. TV - auditory
5. Dream
6. Age regression.

The scale for older children contains one additional item: post-hypnotic suggestion. Both scales can be administered in about twenty minutes. Items are scored pass or fail, and the maximum score for the version of the test for younger children is six, while for the version for older children it is seven.

Stanford Hypnotic Susceptibility Scale, Forms A and B (SHSS: A and B)
This test was devised by Weitzenhoffer and Hilgard (1959), and is designed to be administered individually. The test has two equivalent forms, A and B, the correlation between the two forms averaging 0.83 (Udolf, 1981). It is therefore an ideal device to use when training procedures are used to attempt to alter hypnotic susceptibility, since form A can be used before the training procedure and form B afterwards (or vice versa). Form A contains the following items:

1. Postural sway
2. Eye closure
3. Hand lowering

4. Arm immobilization
5. Finger lock
6. Arm rigidity
7. Hands moving together
8. Verbal inhibition
9. Visual hallucination
10. Eye catalepsy
11. Post-hypnotic suggestion accepted
12. Amnesia

Form B contains essentially similar items, e.g. hands moving apart instead of hands moving together. The test takes about forty-five minutes to administer. One point is given for success on each item, so the maximum score for each form is 12. The items on these scales are generally considered to be quite easy for subjects to achieve, consisting of largely motor rather than cognitive items.

Stanford Hypnotic Susceptibility Scale, Form C (SHSS: C)

This was developed by Weitzenhoffer and Hilgard (1962). It contains 12 items, which are graded in order of difficulty, apart from post-hypnotic amnesia, which although not so hard as some of the other items, must be the last item. However, while the average ranking of a group of subjects might be expected to follow this ordering, a single individual may differ quite dramatically from this order of difficulty. The items are as follows:

1. Hand lowering
2. Moving hands apart
3. Mosquito hallucination
4. Taste hallucination
5. Arm rigidity
6. Dream induction
7. Age regression
8. Arm immobilization
9. Anosmia (loss of smell) to ammonia
10. Hallucinated voice
11. Negative visual hallucination (three boxes)
12. Post-hypnotic amnesia

This form is considered to be much more difficult than forms A and B, containing more cognitive items. It is again scored on a pass/fail basis. It has a split-half reliability coefficient of 0.85, and the same correlation with form A. Test-retest

51

reliability is about 0.85.

Recently Weitzenhoffer (1978a, 1978b) has criticized the Stanford Scales. He believes that they do not give enough weight to the non-volitional nature of response to suggestions, and are hence somewhat misleading as he considers that this is an integral part of the experience of hypnosis. He also raises doubts about the validity of the scales. Bowers (1981) has responded to these criticisms, arguing that neither provides a good enough reason for abandoning the scales.

Stanford Profile Scales of Hypnotic Susceptibility (SPSHS)

This is another individual test, devised by Weitzenhoffer and Hilgard (1967). As its title implies this scale is designed to provide a profile of a person's abilities. It consists of two equivalent forms, I and II, and while just one form may be given, to obtain a full profile of abilities it is recommended that both forms be administered. The induction procedure for form I utilizes arm levitation, and includes the following items:

1. Hand analgesia
2. Hallucination of music (positive)
3. Anosmia to ammonia
4. Recall of a meal of a week or two ago
5. Hallucination of a light
6. Dream about an unspecified subject
7. Agnosia for 'house'
8. Impairment of arithmetic ability
9. Post-hypnotic automatic writing

The type of induction procedure used for form II is based on arm heaviness and lowering. It contains the following items:

1. Heat hallucination
2. Selective deafness
3. Hallucination of ammonia
4. Regression to tenth birthday
5. Negative hallucination of missing watch hand
6. A dream about hypnosis
7. Agnosia for 'scissors'
8. Personality alteration
9. Post-hypnotic automatic writing

Each item on each form is scored on a four point

scale. This profile is generally recognized as containing some very difficult items.

The researcher who is planning to use one of these standardized tests needs to be much more familiar with these tests than is possible from reading the descriptions here. However, there are a few further comments I would like to make which I hope readers will find illuminating.

There is obviously a good argument for tape recording as much of the instructions as possible, so as to ensure that each subject in a particular experiment hears an identical test procedure. However, the problem with this is that the tester then has to interrupt the tape recording if it is felt necessary to respond directly to whatever the subject is doing. I have found this occasionally necessary when a subject has appeared to be showing some signs of distress at some of the items on the tests. For instance, one subject became very anxious when she found herself unable to utter her name (item eight of the SHSS). Certainly it would not be surprising if some of the items on these tests did cause anxiety, particularly as these tests are usually administered with far less preparation of the subject than would be the case in an experimental or clinical setting where hypnosis is used.

As already indicated, some of the scales are more difficult than others. A comparison of the SHSS:A and the SHSS:C should make this clear. Hilgard and Hilgard (1983) have produced figures indicating that about 11 per cent of subjects score 11-12 on the SHSS:A, 21 per cent score 8-10, 27 per cent score 5-7 and 41 per cent score 0-4. Wagstaff (1981) quotes corresponding figures for the SHSS:C of 6 per cent, 18 per cent, 30 per cent and 46 per cent. Clearly the SHSS:C is more difficult, almost half the subjects being classified as of low susceptibility.

The final point I wish to make here is that it is dangerous to assume that someone who scores high on one of the scales is going to be good in every area. Similarly, someone with a low score may yet be very proficient in one particular area. This is what the SPSHS:I and II are designed to find out. Just as intelligence may be usefully conceptualized as having different components, so hypnotic ability often seems to be made up of various components, some individuals being more proficient in some areas than others.

CORRELATES OF HYPNOTIZABILITY

It would seem reasonable to assume that hypnotizability, particularly if it is at least in part a relatively stable personality dimension itself, might have some correlates. Perhaps before exploring this issue it would be worth considering whether or not hypnotizability is a relatively stable phenomenon. Morgan, Johnson and Hilgard (1974) state that after an interval of ten years a group of subjects retested showed a correlation of 0.6 with their original score. However, this does not mean that hypnotizability cannot be altered. There have been many attempts to increase hypnotizability, using various techniques, including operant conditioning techniques (Delprato and Holmes, 1978; Katz, 1979), sensory deprivation (Sanders and Reyher, 1969), muscle tone feedback (Wickramasekera, 1973). There seems no doubt that many are successful.

However, deciding what was really responsible for the increase is often extremely difficult. Even where a control group is used extreme care must be taken to ensure that the control group is identical in every way with the experimental group, e.g. in terms of attention given to them, confidence of the experimenter, as well as the more mundane matter of having matching subjects. Furthermore, it is not always clear what should happen to the control group, and different researchers differ in their opinions concerning the adequacy of various matching techniques. The general opinion (Wagstaff, 1981; Diamond, 1982) is that hypnotizability can be increased by training, although it is not always clear what aspect of the training has been responsible for the increase.

Since we have been examining the stability of hypnotizability, it seems appropriate to examine the relationship between hypnotizability and age.

Age

Bowers (1976) is careful to draw a distinction between the stability of hypnotic susceptibility and its development. The study by Morgan et al. (1974) mentioned above points to some stability over time, but it is also possible to point to some evidence which appears to show age-related increases and decreases in hypnotic susceptibility. London (1965) found that children of age seven and above tend to be good subjects. Until about age fourteen susceptibility increases, after which it starts to decrease gradually, as it continues to do throughout the adult's life. Morgan and Hilgard (1973) using the SHSS:A found that nine to twelve seemed to be the most susceptible age group, with those over forty the least susceptible. These two studies seem broadly in agreement.

Wagstaff (1981) argues that these changes may be due in part to changes in rigidity, trust and compliance. If there is any physiological base to hypnosis, then such changes could be due to physiological changes which take place during development and ageing. There again, the changes could be due to psychological changes which take place as part of development throughout the entire lifespan.

Heritability

There is little evidence that hypnotic susceptibility may have a genetic component. Morgan (1973) provides evidence which indicates a genetic component, but this study has not been replicated. Furthermore, there may be methodological problems with the type of experimental design employed. When dealing with such a complex phenomenon as hypnotic susceptibility a strong genetic component would seem unlikely.

Sex

Folklore holds that females are more susceptible than males, but the evidence does not appear to support this. Fellows (1979), using the BSS reports that the sex of the subjects was not related to their suggestibility, nor was the sex of the experimenter. This appears to be in line with previous findings (Barber, 1965; Hilgard, 1965). However, he does discuss the possibility of an interaction effect between the sex of the experimenter and the sex of the subject, female subjects exhibiting slightly greater susceptibility with male experimenters.

Physiological Measures

By having the variables of sex and age outside this heading I do not wish to imply that they do not have a physiological basis. Rather I am using the term 'physiological' in a narrower context, which I hope will become clear as we proceed.

Bakan (1969), Gur and Gur (1974), Morgan, Macdonald and Hilgard (1974) and Sackeim (1982) support the hypothesis that among right handers the hypnotic state produces more activation in the right cerebral hemisphere than in the left, but whether this indicates a genuine increase in right hemisphere activity or a suppression of left hemisphere activity is open to question. Several lines of research support this idea. Morgan et al. (1974) found that the alpha wave component of EEG under hypnosis was more akin to that produced by right hemispheric spatial tasks than left hemispheric verbal tasks. Frumkin, Ripley and Cox (1978) observed a lessening of the right ear advantage for speech under hypnosis, which reflects the left hemisphere's superior ability in this task. Tellegen and Atkinson (1974) and Hilgard (1979) discuss the greater imaginative involvement (generally associated with the right hemisphere) among subjects with high hypnotic susceptibility. Sackeim (1981) concludes that right handers generally respond more to hypnotic suggestions involving the left side of the body than the right side of the body.

However, these issues are complicated by some other findings. Gur and Gur (1974, and Birkett (1979) found that only right handed males exhibited the tendency to move their eyes to the left under hypnosis. For left handed males and right handed females there is no apparent preferred direction of movement, while for left handed females eye movement is to the right. It is difficult to explain these findings, but it is important to remember that there are degrees of handedness, and that handedness does not always reflect cerebral dominance. Morgan et al. (1974) found no evidence of greater alpha activity in the right hemisphere in subjects with high susceptibility in comparison with subjects with low susceptibility, which is perhaps contrary to expectations.

At the present time no physiological measures seem to have been isolated which reliably predict hypnotizability. There are tantalizing hints that handedness, sex and alpha EEG activity may have some predictive ability, but the precise nature of the relationship between the variables eludes us at present.

Personality Measures
A large number of correlations between personality

tests and hypnotic susceptibility have been reported by Hilgard (1968). Most of these are not significant. However, there do appear to be some personality correlates of hypnotic susceptibility, albeit weak ones. Hilgard and Bentler (1963) report a correlation of 0.21 between extraversion and susceptibility, while Gibson and Curran (1974) and Gibson and Corcoran (1975) found somewhat different results, which indicated that stable extraverts and neurotic introverts tend to be more susceptible than stable intoverts and neurotic extraverts, while Barber (1964) concluded that there was no relationship. Wagstaff (1981) discusses a number of studies which indicate a small positive correlation between 'influencability' or conformity and hypnotic susceptibility.

Apart from the studies of imaginative involvement mentioned in the previous section, there seem to be no other personality correlates of hypnotic susceptibility. As Bowers (1976) points out, this is not really surprising. Different aspects of personality tend to manifest themselves in different situations, which may account for some researchers finding a correlation between hypnotic susceptibility and one particular aspect of personality, only for other researchers to fail to confirm this. It may also be the case that hypnotic susceptibility is not a unitary phenomenon, but is comprised of a number of interacting components which are present in varying degrees in particular individuals, and manifest themselves in different ways in different situations.

Barber (1964) reports that some subjects are 'better' subjects with some hypnotists than others, and it is to be expected that the better the rapport between hypnotist and subject, the more hypnotizable the subject should prove. Barber and Calverley (1962) note that hypnotizability is high if the subject has a strong motivation for being hypnotized and a positive attitude towards hypnosis, and that hypnotizability is low if the subject holds the opposite views. Melei and Hilgard (1964) found this characteristic was more enhanced in female subjects.

PERSONAL REFLECTIONS

Despite the amount of work which has been carried out on susceptibility tests and potential correlates of hypnotizability, the best method for determining whether individuals are of low, medium, or high hypnotizability is to hypnotize them. However, by saying this I do not mean to devalue any of the work carried out on either susceptibility tests or possible correlates. On the contrary, it is very valuable and informative work. The problems occur when hypnotists use susceptibility tests and correlates in appropriate contexts.

For instance, the greatest care has to be taken in deciding not to hypnotize a particular person on the basis of a standardized personality test. Although the person may have a low score on the test overall, there may still be particular areas of ability which can be used by the skilful hypnotist. In the case of possible correlates of hypnosis, even if a particular personality dimension were found to have a high correlation with hypnotizability, to reject any one individual on the basis of a particular score on this personality dimension would be rather foolish. Although it might be expected that this individual might have low hypnotizability, this person might be the statistical exception.

The situations where correlates and susceptibility tests are useful is generally in research, and where the hypnotist considers it is important to keep records of scores on, for instance, the SHSS:C. To use susceptibility scores to select a group of subjects for an experiment is fine. Not to attempt hypnosis with an individual, particularly when hypnosis is considered to be a valuable adjunct to therapy, on the basis of a susceptibility score alone, is not very sensible.

SELECTED READING

Bowers, K. S. (1976) <u>Hypnosis for the Seriously Curious</u>, Brooks/Cole Publishing Company, Monterey, California
Chapters five, six and seven provide a first-class survey of many of the areas relating to hypnotic susceptibility.

Hilgard, E. R. (1965) <u>Hypnotic Susceptibility</u>, Harcourt Brace and World, New York
This is a classic which is still worth reading.

Hull, C. L. (1933) <u>Hypnosis and Susceptibility: An Experimental Approach</u>, Appleton-Century-Crofts, New York
Even more of a classic, the first book to approach hypnosis from a psychological-scientific background.

Wagstaff, G. F. (1981) **Hypnosis, Compliance and Belief**, The Harvester Press, Brighton
Chapter seven is an excellent discussion of many of the factors relating to hypnotic susceptibility.

Chapter Five

HYPNOTIC INDUCTION TECHNIQUES

It is perhaps unfortunate that hypnosis is referred to as being 'induced'. Linguistically convenient as it is to speak of inducing hypnosis, its implication that hypnotic subjects are passive individuals who have hypnotic experiences thrust upon them is simply not the case. The role of the hypnotist is to set up the conditions necessary for hypnosis and hypnotic experiences to occur, but it is the subject who in the end is responsible for what actually occurs. This is in line too with the work of Barber (1969) where he outlines the antecedent variables he believes affect subjects' responses and experiences.

It follows from this that hypnosis is not a battle of wills, nor is it necessary for the hypnotist to be a dynamic, forceful character. What is required is for the hypnotist to establish a good rapport with the client. A climate of dislike and perhaps even mistrust is one in which hypnosis is almost guaranteed to fail, as indeed would any co-operative venture. The process of hypnotic induction can usefully be viewed as a situation in which the subject co-operates with the hypnotist, and this co-operation can be withheld if the subject wishes.

Also of importance is whether the induction procedure is really necessary for the experience of phenomena usually associated with hypnosis. Some of the evidence relating to this was discussed in Chapter Two in relation to the work of Barber (1969, 1979). In an attempt to throw further light on related issues we will examine the work of Orne (1959) and his development of the simulating paradigm. This paradigm is really quite simple. Some subjects are instructed to fake (simulate) being hypnotized, while others are given no such instructions. The simulating subjects are told that the hypnotist does not know which subjects are genuine and which are faking, and as long as the experiment is not stopped they are succeeding in fooling the hypnotist. Neither are they told how to fake; that is left to their own discretion. In practice the simulating group are often subjects with low hypnotic susceptibility, to minimize the chance of them actually being hypnotized.

The results of these simulating paradigm experiments are clear; hypnosis can be successfully faked. However, the interpretation of this finding is not so clear. Although the two groups of subjects are indistinguishable by the experimenter on the basis of overt responses, and even continue the deception when they are asked after the hypnotic session whether they were hypnotized or not, their subjective experiences may of course have been quite different. Sheehan (1973) has also found that the instructions given to the subjects are important as this can vary their simulating ability, as can the composition of the simulating group. There is also a problem in that the two groups are not matched, one group typically scoring high on hypnotic susceptibility tests, the other group scoring low. It may be that low scorers are more motivated to fake hypnotic phenomena than high scorers. It may also be the case that high scorers cannot fake hypnosis because they cannot resist being hypnotized if they are trying to comply with the experimenters requests. Finally, the fact that some subjects are capable of faking does not mean that all hypnotic behaviour is faked. Although we can wield Occam's razor and argue that since in many cases hypnotic phenomena can be produced by non-hypnotized persons, perhaps hypnosis is not necessary to explain 'hypnotic-like' phenomena, it must be remembered that nature is not always so parsimonious as the scientist.

From the point of view of the hypnotist who is trying to tell whether or not a particular person is hypnotized this may seem rather depressing. There are certain signs, however, which indicate that an individual may be hypnotized. They do not conclusively prove that this is the case, but their presence, particularly if corroborated by subjects' subjective reports does allow all but the most sceptical to at least hold that it is a possibility.

Udolf (1981) gives a list of signs which he believes are likely to indicate hypnosis, although as he points out there is likely to be large individual variation. I have omitted signs which require physiological measuring devices from the list for two reasons. The first is that such devices are often not available, and the second is that often far too much weight is given to physiological evidence in situations where the reliability of the data does not permit it. Relatively simple observations seem far less susceptible to this complication. These signs are also more appropriate to situations where 'sleepy-type' hypnotic induction procedures have been used. Six signs are given:

1. Fluttering of the eyelids followed by eye closure.
2. Often signs of quite profound relaxation, e.g. limpness of limbs, lack of facial expression, little or no spontaneous speech, and often pauses before questions are answered.
3. Subjects may often interpret instructions literally.
4. There may be excessive salivation or swallowing.
5. The subject's breathing often becomes observably slower and deeper.
6. The subject is more suggestible.

HYPNOTIC INDUCTION PROCEDURES

There are a large number of hypnotic induction techniques, in fact almost as many as there are hypnotists! The ones I am including in this chapter are, I hope, a representative sample, although no doubt many readers will find their own favourite omitted. I am not greatly in favour of reading induction techniques verbatim from books, believing it best to tailor the induction procedure to the particular individual. For those who would like to see exactly how induction procedures look, Hartland (1971) provides a good introduction.

Braidism
As its name suggests this is a technique based on a method used by James Braid (1846). Although Braid's belief that muscular fatigue of the eye muscles can in some ways produce an hypnotic state (see Chapter One for more details) is now generally considered erroneous, Braidism is often used for inducing hypnosis.
   In this technique the hypnotist instructs the subject to look at a point high on the ceiling or

high up on the wall. The point should be high enough
for it to be above the subject's line of vision. The
hypnotist then suggests that the subject's eyelids
are getting heavy. This feeling is likely to be
enhanced by the discomfort of the suggested line of
vision. A good hypnotist will also reinforce the
eyelid flutterings which the subject naturally
makes, suggesting that the subject's eyelids are
wanting to close (note the non-volitional nature of
the suggestion). In my experience some naive
subjects respond to this very rapidly (fifteen
seconds or less), while others may take up to five
minutes. Subjects who have previously been
instructed to enter hypnosis when given a particular
signal will close their eyes immediately. Once the
subject's eyes are closed other suggestions can be
given.

This is perhaps the simplest of the many
variations of this technique. Others involve asking
the subject to stare at a torch, a candle flame, a
spinning disk, and even at the hypnotist's eyes.
This last conjures up the idea of hypnotic induction
involving a battle of wills, a totally false idea,
and as such is not recommended. Braidism is also
similar to the technique so beloved of old (and not
so old) movies, inducing hypnosis by having the
subjects stare at a watch swinging to and fro in
front of them.

Another variation which is often used involves
a distraction technique, and is often referred to as
'eye fixation with distraction'. The eye fixation
part of the technique is as above, but the subject
is also required to count, perhaps normally, or
perhaps starting at five hundred and subtracting
three each time. It is argued that this
concentration on a particular repetitive task aids
the induction procedure by preventing the subjects
thinking about anything more interesting.

Arm Levitation

In this method hypnosis is induced by having the
subjects raise their arms in response to
suggestions, and they are told that when their arm
is, for instance, shoulder high, they will be
hypnotized. As with all methods of hypnotic
induction, it is important to explain to the
subjects what is going to happen before the
induction procedure begins. It would be rather
foolish of the hypnotist for the subjects to raise
their hands shoulder-high yet fail to be hypnotized

because they were not told this was the goal of the exercise. (Note how the subjects' expectations determine how they interpret their experience).

As always it is important to ensure that the subjects are in a comfortable position. They can also be informed that they can change their position, scratch themselves, cough, etc. during the session without it adversely affecting their hypnotic state. The hypnotist then informs the subjects roughly what to expect, and asks them to concentrate on the sensations they will experience in their arm. Suggestions are then given that the arm will feel lighter and lighter, and as it gets light it will float up into the air. Various types of imagery can be suggested. e.g. a magnet drawing the hand upwards, or a lighter-than-air balloon attached to it. Little twitches of the arm can be reinforced. If the arm does not rise, the hypnotist can raise it physically, saying that it just needs to be started, and then it will really go. Once arm levitation is accomplished it is generally best to suggest that the subjects remain hypnotized while their arms return to a more comfortable position. It is often quite surprising for the inexperienced hypnotist to observe the tremendous individual variation in the speed of arm levitation. Some subjects are extremely fast, while others are much slower, some wave their arms about while they are rising, while others keep them almost rigid.

There are many variations on this theme. Arm lowering is one, and while this is almost always successful in the sense that the arm lowers, it does not always seem very convincing to say to the subjects that when their arms are resting on their knees they will be hypnotized. Hands together is an alternative method in which subjects are asked to hold their hands out with their palms facing each other, about a foot apart. Suggestions are then given that the hands are slowly coming together, and when the palms touch hypnosis will be induced. No doubt readers will be able to think of many variations for themselves which are likely to be equally effective.

The Miller Endogenic Method
This is a method first demonstrated by Miller in 1958, and described in detail in a later publication (1979). Here is the description Miller (1979, pp. 89-90) gives to clients who want an explanation of the induction method:

He is told (1) that slow, deep respiration will cause an oxygen overload in the bloodstream; (2) that this overload will affect the respiratory center in the medulla, causing a marked change in his breathing rhythm with a slowing of the heart and respiration, relaxing the entire mind and body progressively; (3) that this effect will spread quite rapidly from the hind brain over the mid and fore brain, inducing a very pleasant progressive relaxation of mind and body; and (4) that he will feel drowsy and sleepy but at no time will he lose contact with the therapist. He will be able to hear the therapist's voice and to express himself freely and without effort.

Five phases are outlined in Miller's description of the technique. The first phase involves telling the client to breathe slowly and deeply, and to watch for three test signs. These are: (1) chest breathing changing to belly breathing, (2) belly breathing becoming shallower and levelling off, and (3) head movement, the direction of which depends upon initial head orientation (an alternative sign is toe deviation, either inwards or outwards, depending again on their initial orientation).

Phase two involves telling the client the first part of the test has been passed, and that tranquil feelings, a sense of well-being and comfort will diffuse throughout the mind and body. The client is also told that drowsiness will become more pronounced, breathing almost imperceptible, and muscle relaxation progressively deeper.

Phase three utilizes a count procedure. Miller recommends starting at thirty and counting in reverse order to one, suggesting deeper relaxation with each number. However at nineteen the count is reversed and goes back up to twenty-nine, although the client is still told that each number indicates deeper relaxation. Then what Miller (1979, p. 92) terms double reversal occurs, and the count goes back down to one.

In phase four the hypnotist raises each arm and leg in turn, and then lets it drop. The client is told that lifting each arm (or leg) tests the depth of the hypnotic trance, and dropping the arm (or leg) deepens it still further.

The final phase makes use of the hand levitation technique. The client is informed that a helium balloon is being attached to the wrist, and that this will lift the hand up in a smooth sweep until it makes contact with the forehead. The client is told that when this contact is made a deep and beautiful trance will be apparent throughout the whole body, and the hand will sink slowly down again, and the trance will become even deeper.

This is obviously quite a lengthy induction procedure. However, the hypnotic state brought about should be quite profound, for it can be argued that much of the induction procedure is really a deepening procedure. As I will attempt to show later, the distinction between an induction and a deepening procedure is not always easy to make.

Spiegel Eye-Roll Levitation Technique

A detailed description of this technique can be found in Spiegel (1976). In this, subjects are first instructed to look upwards, and then keeping their eyes rolled upwards to close their eyes. They are then told to take a deep breath, hold it, then exhale and at the same time relax their eyes and let their bodies float. The next stage is arm levitation, which involves stroking each finger in turn while suggesting that the hand is getting lighter all the time. The trance is terminated by touching the left elbow.

Progressive Relaxation

This is generally considered to be a very time consuming procedure. In essence the hypnotist suggests that each muscle group is relaxing in turn, and the relaxation is spreading from one muscle group to the other. Some hypnotists prefer to work from the head down, others from the feet up. My own preference is for the latter. It is possible to make use of Jacobson's technique (1938, 1962) and have the subject tense each muscle group in turn before relaxing them. By this means the feeling of muscle relaxation is normally more profound, because of course, when sitting in a chair many muscles are relaxed anyway. I have found this technique quite effective, particularly when followed by arm levitation, or another deepening procedure.

Some hypnotists use the relaxation technique with clients they believe would react badly to the word 'hypnosis'. (One hopes it would not be used at all if there was any possibility that clients would respond badly to the experience of hypnosis). Clearly there is an ethical problem here which hypnotists must resolve in accord with their own principles. While there can be virtually no distinction between the performance of a relaxation procedure as a means of inducing hypnosis and as a means of inducing relaxation, the type of procedures carried out after this may vary quite dramatically depending on whether the therapist is using relaxation as an independent technique or as a means of inducing hypnosis. The moral dilemma for the hypnotist lies in choosing between misleading clients or withholding from them a potentially beneficial form of treatment. While I accept that it may not work in every case, I believe that careful preparation of the subject may go a long way towards alleviating worries and objections about hypnosis. I am sure that most readers would agree that therapeutic relationships cannot grow and flourish where deception is present.

Chiasson's Technique
This is quite a straight-forward technique, more details of which can be found in Chiasson (1964). Subjects are instructed to place their hands about twelve inches in front of their faces, palm outwards. The elbow should be bent, and the fingers together. Subjects are instructed to watch their hands, and as they watch them their fingers will slowly begin to spread and their hands will move towards them. When their hands touch their faces, their eyes will close, if they have not already done so. They are also told that as soon as this happens they will be completely relaxed, their hands will fall gently to rest in a comfortable position, and the relaxation will become deeper.

Flower's Method
Udolf (1981) believes this to be one of the most stereotyped methods of induction. Subjects are asked to look 'into the distance', not at any particular point. The hypnotist then informs subjects that as the hypnotist counts slowly up to a particular number (perhaps twenty), on each count they will close their eyes and then open them again. Each time this action is performed subjects are told they will find it harder and harder to open their eyes, until at some point during the count, and certainly by the time the count reaches twenty, the subjects will be unable to open their eyes. Once this happens subjects are given suggestions of trance deepening.

There are several variations on this technique. For instance the number twenty may be varied, or no number may be named at all, subjects simply being informed that in a short while during the counting their eyes will remain closed. Another variation is to use a rhythmic mechanical device, e.g. a clock with a loud tick, or better still a metronome. Another related technique which is really quite a significant variation is to suggest that on odd numbers the subjects close their eyes and on even numbers open them, and by the time the count reaches a specified odd number the subjects no longer have any desire to open them. It is also possible to give suggestions of relaxation during the counting procedure, but this does have the effect of breaking up the rhythm.

Sacerdote's Sculpture Technique

This is a technique described by Sacerdote (1970). Subjects are asked to raise their non-dominant hands to a position where they can view them comfortably. The hypnotist then describes the hand as if it were a piece of sculpture, emphasizing the shape, texture, smoothness, symmetry etc. There are considerable pauses between these observations to allow the subjects time for reflection. It is suggested that at some point the subjects' eyes might close as they reflect on their hands, or possibly on a favourite sculpture or painting. When this happens the subjects will feel more relaxed still and their hands will gradually fall to rest on their laps.

Cognitive (Imagery) Methods

The basic technique here is to describe to subjects a vivid picture of a particular scene, e.g. a seashore, mountain pasture, garden etc., making use of as many sensory modalities as possible. Kroger and Fezler (1976) provide a number of such word pictures. While subjects are concentrating on imagining this scene, suggestions of relaxation are made. It is always worth discussing the imagery beforehand with the subject, so as to be certain that the subject likes the suggested scene. It is no good suggesting a stroll on a river-bank to someone who has a phobia about water, unless of course, the induction is part of a therapeutic procedure for the phobic object.

Written Techniques
In cases where spoken induction procedures cannot be used, for instance with deaf subjects, other methods may be employed. One of these is a written technique. Many of the above methods are adaptable for this purpose, for instance, the imagery technique immediately above.

Pantomime Techniques
Erickson (1964), probably one of the most inventive of all hypnotists, developed a number of methods using sign language, touching and other gestures for subjects who are deaf or language-impaired. In addition there may be cases in which it would be appropriate to use these techniques for subjects who did not have any such impairment.

Observation (Chaperon) Techniques
This is another technique of Erickson's, (Erickson, Rossi and Rossi, 1976) in which the subject is hypnotized as a result of watching another person being hypnotized. This is a technique which Erickson used for clients who he believed would respond better if they were unaware they were being hypnotized. It is possible to raise ethical objections again here, and again it must be left to therapists to solve this moral dilemma for themselves.

Erickson's Naturalistic Techniques
Many references to these techniques can be found throughout Erickson's work, e.g. Erickson (1958). These techniques generally involve asking the subject to fixate on something, and then the hypnotist talks about the subject's physiological processes, e.g. heart rate, respiration rate, and suggests that the subject is aware of them changing. Often the next step is to suggest that the subject is thinking about something that happened during childhood, and to contrast mental experience then with the subject's mental experience now. These techniques are often quite individual, and require a great deal of skill on the part of the hypnotist to carry them out. They are also very rewarding for the hypnotist.

Rehearsal Technique

This is sometimes recommended for subjects who are very apprehensive about hypnosis. Subjects are asked if they would like to rehearse the hypnotic induction technique before actually being hypnotized. Sometimes hypnosis may occur during the rehearsal. If this happens the hypnotist should be careful to adhere to the outline of the session if one was agreed with the subjects.

Mechanical Aids

There are a number of mechanical devices which can be used in the hypnotic induction procedure. Some of these, like the metronome, were not designed specifically for it, whereas others, like the hypnodisc, were. Anything which provides a rhythmic beat may be useful, given the appropriate hypnotic 'chatter', and hypnodiscs or lights may provide a suitable fixation point. Chevreul pendulums and pocket watches have already been mentioned. Another method which was once popular is the 'Hand of God' technique. This induction procedure requires an electric shock generator capable of producing a mild electric shock. The subject holds one handle, the hypnotist the other. The hypnotist tells the subject that when the hypnotist touches the subject's forehead, a strange tingling sensation will result, (caused by the completion of the electrical circuit), and the subject will enter a trance. I have tried this, both as hypnotist and subject, and a trance has never been the result, only a headache!

Tape recordings and video recordings are other devices which can be used. They are very useful for carrying out standardized induction procedures, but they cannot of course be easily altered to take account of the subject's responses. A tape recording of background music or waves breaking on the seashore is sometimes useful for initially putting the subject at ease, and may even be useful if continued throughout the hypnotic session.

'Touching' Techniques

These have already been mentioned in relation to Erickson's work. Techniques involving stroking the patient's limbs and face date back at least as far as Mesmer, and at that time were thought necessary to ensure a proper flow of animal magnetism. Many induction techniques require the hypnotist to touch lightly the client's body, usually the fingers, hand or wrist. There seems to be no evidence to suggest that stroking techniques are more effective than verbal techniques. Since it has been argued that erotic sensations can result from such stroking, or that the intentions of the hypnotist can be misconstrued, the hypnotist should be very careful when using techniques involving touching.

Instant Hypnosis
The idea of instant hypnosis is one which occurs very frequently in the cinema, and is perpetuated by stage hypnotists. However, instant hypnosis does not happen quite as easily as those agencies would have us believe. Rather there are certain circumstances under which hypnosis may occur, or appear to occur. One of these is when subjects are given a post-hypnotic suggestion that they will be re-hypnotized following a certain cue. Another is when dealing with subjects who are extremely responsive to suggestions, who may become quite deeply hypnotized almost as soon as the induction procedure has begun. A third circumstance is that when observing stage hypnotists it is not always apparent that the subjects are sometimes already hypnotized before the audience sees them. On some occasions too the stage hypnotist is able to induce and deepen the trance while ostensibly talking to the audience.

Alert Hypnosis
In contrast to the normal 'sleepy-type' induction procedures, an 'alert-type' induction procedure may also be used. Vingoe (1968, 1973) has described a technique in which feelings of body relaxation and mind alertness are suggested to subjects. Banyai and Hilgard (1976) reported a particularly interesting technique in which subjects were given suggestions of alertness while riding an exercise cycle to ensure that they did not become physically relaxed. No differences in hypnotic responsiveness were found between the two conditions. Fellows (1984) reports that Banyai and her workers are continuing their investigations in this area in Hungary.

HYPNOTIC INDUCTION TECHNIQUES FOR CHILDREN

Many of the techniques described above are perfectly suitable for children, although it may be necessary to alter the language used so it is age appropriate. Children may also need a different type of explanation of the nature of hypnosis, and what they are likely to experience. Particularly suitable techniques are those involving imagery, which may come through fairy tales, television programmes, or songs. Olness and Gardner (1981) list a number of different induction techniques which can be used with children of different ages.

As I have already argued, the behaviour of hypnotized individuals is at least partly determined by their culturally based expectations. Children often have fewer expectations concerning hypnosis, and because of this there is usually more variation in their behaviour. Children are likely to be much more active during the hypnotic session, and to cough, giggle, move around, etc.

Hypnosis with children generally presents few problems. What is important is that the hypnotist has a background of working with children so as to better understand their fears and problems. It is the general treatment and understanding of children which requires much skill and knowledge; the hypnotic techniques are relatively straight forward.

DEEPENING TECHNIQUES

Deepening techniques are employed in order to deepen the hypnotic trance. However, it would be a mistake to believe that induction techniques induced hypnosis and then deepening techniques took over, for, as will be obvious from the above discussion, induction techniques also have the effect of deepening the hypnotic experience. Despite this, a hypnotist may feel that a particular subject would benefit from a deepening technique. My own opinion is that any suggestion which hypnotized subjects follow, is likely to deepen their hypnotic trance. However there are some particular deepening techniques, often involving imagery, which are frequently used.

Simple counting may be used, with the suggestion that the subject will go deeper into the trance as the hypnotist says each number. This is perhaps more effective when combined with an imagery technique. There are lots of natural situations which can be utilized for this, and one should be selected with the subject beforehand. The imagery of lifts going down is quite popular, but subjects do not always like lifts, which is why it is important to check with them beforehand. If it is acceptable to them then it is quite straightforward to make suggestions that as the lift goes down they are going deeper and deeper into the trance, counting off the floors at the same time.

My own preference is for scenes which can utilize all the sensory modalities, which does not readily evoke pleasant imagery with lifts! Walking down a hill is a situation which can be easily used as a deepening technique, and plenty of pleasant sensory information can be suggested to the subject.

One of my favourites is the sunken garden. In this subjects are asked to imagine they are in a garden, that the sun is shining, the birds are singing, there is a gentle background buzz of bees among the flowers, the scent of blossom is in the air, and they can feel the ground soft beneath their feet. (Note how as many sensory modalities as possible are being used). Once this scene has been set, subjects are guided through the garden until they come to some steps going down to a sunken garden. It is suggested that going down the steps represents going deeper into the hypnotic trance. At the bottom of the steps I usually request the subjects to take a few steps to where there is a pool of still, clear water. This pool can be used in two ways. I suggest that it is a magic pool in which they either see whatever I suggest, or that they see something which is particularly important to them, and I ask them to describe this to me.

Another scene I use quite often is that of the seashore. Again the sound of the waves breaking on the beach, the warmth of the sun, the cry of the seagulls, and the feel of the sand between their toes all provide a wealth of sensory imagery. I usually suggest that subjects concentrate on their footsteps, and as they take each step and feel each foot sink a little into the sand so they can feel themselves sinking deeper and deeper into the hypnotic trance.

Clearly, many scenes can be used as deepening procedures, and often new ones, or interesting variations on old themes, can be worked out with the help of the subject.

There are a number of scales which were designed to measure trance depth. One of the oldest is the Davis-Husband Scale of Hypnotic Susceptibility, which assumes five depth levels. These are: insusceptible, hypnoidal, light trance, medium trance, and deep trance or somnambulism. Each of these levels contains certain responses the hypnotist should look for which are thought characteristic of that particular level. A light trance may be characterized by relaxation, eye closure, slowing of muscular activity, and ability to perform simple post-hypnotic suggestions. In a medium trance the following may be observed: glove anaesthesia, partial amnesia, catalepsy of entire skeletal structure and personality changes. A deep trance would be characterized by: ability to open eyes without affecting the trance, post-hypnotic anaesthesia, conformity to bizarre post-hypnotic suggestions, positive and negative visual and auditory hallucinations and subjective feelings of detachment. Subjects are scored for each of these items. Scores of zero or one represent insusceptible subjects, scores between two and five hypnoidal subjects, scores between six and twelve light trance subjects, scores between thirteen and twenty medium trance subjects, and scores between twenty-one and thirty deep trance subjects.

LeCron and Bordeaux have produced a more detailed scale containing fifty items, the subject getting a score of two for each item passed. Not only are some of the items within each level of trance different, an extra level of trance is given, called a plenary trance. This is described as a stuporous condition in which all spontaneous activity is inhibited. Further details of these scales can be found in Ehrenreich (1963) and LeCron and Bordeaux (1949).

One problem which is probably already apparent with these scales is the time taken to note all the characteristics. While this is not a problem for detailed investigations into trance depth, where a therapist wants a quick indication of trance depth they are rather too cumbersome. An alternative technique is to ask subjects to estimate their level of trance depth on a scale where, for instance, zero is perfectly normal, and twenty is a very deep level. Tart's work has already been mentioned in this context, and Tart (1978) provides a useful starting point for this work.

AWAKENING

In one sense it is rather foolish to talk about awakening since it implies that the hypnotised person is asleep, and we have already seen that this is not so. However, it is a convenient word to use to refer to a situation which looks remarkably like waking up, so I will continue to use it. Normally at the end of the hypnotic session the hypnotist terminates the trance. However, as Orne and Evans (1966), and Evans and Orne (1971) have shown, if the hypnotist just leaves the room the subject will awaken after a few minutes. Despite this, most hypnotists choose to terminate the trance themselves!

This can be done simply by instructing the subject to awaken, but not unnaturally most subjects prefer a gradual awakening. This can be done using a counting technique, suggesting that as the count proceeds the subjects will become more and more awake, and by the final number is reached their eyes will be open and they will be fully awake. This count need not be very long, five numbers is quite adequate. Some hypnotists prefer to count down to one, others go the other way. As far as I am aware there is no evidence that one is preferable to the other.

Many subjects express a reluctance to wake up, which is not surprising, for it is generally a pleasant and relaxing experience. However a failure to awaken is extremely rare and generally the result of the hypnotist confusing the subject who takes literally something the hypnotist meant only metaphorically. I know of no authenticated case where a normal subject has been impossible to awaken. (Although I am sure someone will now inform me of one).

PREPARATION OF THE SUBJECT AND RUNNING THE SESSION

Adequate preparation of the subject is essential to get the most possible from the hypnotic session. Obviously the type of preparation depends on how well the hypnotist and subject know each other, on the subject's knowledge of hypnosis, and on the purpose of the hypnotic session (research or clinical). As has already been indicated, a good rapport between the hypnotist and subject helps. When I meet a new subject one of my first aims is to find out what they know about hypnosis and to try to

correct any misconceptions they may have. Udolf
(1981) lists nine misconceptions concerning
hypnosis, and I have met potential subjects who have
held all nine! This is not too surprising given that
most people's experiences of hypnosis are limited
to stage hypnotists and sensationalized stories
about the use of hypnosis in solving crimes, of
which more later.

I also like to let the subjects ask me
questions about hypnosis, as this often reveals
particular aspects of hypnosis that they are worried
about. Generally I ask them if they would like to do
an informal susceptibility test, perhaps the body
sway test, to give them some experience of
responding to suggestions. At this point I generally
ask them to remove contact lenses if they are
wearing them, as I believe that these may be
uncomfortable.

Obviously precisely how much is revealed to the
subjects concerning the hypnotic session depends on
how much the hypnotist believes can be revealed
without jeopardizing the research or therapy. I
generally draw up a brief schedule which I go
through with the subjects, so they are prepared as
far as possible for what is to happen. A typical
schedule to demonstrate the experience of hypnosis
to subjects would be as follows:

1. Induction procedure (relaxation)
2. Deepening technique involving imagery
   (sunken garden)
3. Arm levitation (to give experience of non-
   volitional movement)
4. Age regression
5. Sensation of warmth in one hand
6. Post-hypnotic suggestion
7. Awakening

Often subjects ask what they will feel like, and
then the hypnotist has to be careful not to suggest
specific details for fear of biasing the subjects'
own experiences. On the other hand, if the hypnotist
wishes the subject to experience a particular
feeling this suggestion will work to advantage.

Once the session gets under way, I am careful
to try to ensure that subjects have only pleasant
experiences by emphasizing the pleasant aspects of
the experiences. For instance, during arm levitation
I usually say something to the effect that although
it seems strange for your arm to be moving of its
own accord, it feels quite pleasant, and you are

glad you are able to experience it. I try to maintain this pleasant feeling for subjects even after the end of the hypnotic session, by suggesting that when they awaken they will feel pleasantly refreshed and relaxed.

Some hypnotists include a post-hypnotic suggestion that subjects will only be hypnotized by that particular hypnotist, or members of that particular profession. One hopes that this reflects a genuine concern for the patient rather than a desire to increase either the hypnotist's or the profession's revenue. Whatever the reason, as Gibson (1981) points out, to leave your dentist with a post-hypnotic suggestion that only members of certain professions can hypnotize you is an unnecessary restriction, and also seems to me rather unethical. If hypnotists wish to safeguard their subjects from being hypnotized in certain circumstances there are many suitable forms of words which can be used. I have found that subjects are sometimes reassured if they are given a post-hypnotic suggestion to the effect that they will only be hypnotized by people they trust and never against their will, or unknowingly. Although I think their need for reassurance reflects a mistaken view of the possibilities of hypnosis, as one subject told me, 'that's really put my mind at ease'.

After the hypnotic session I discuss the subjects' experiences with them. I think this is vital as often the subjects reveal interesting pieces of information, and, particularly if it is their first experience of hypnosis, are very eager to discuss what happened.

SELF-HYPNOSIS

Self-hypnosis, or autohypnosis as it is often called, involves individuals hypnotizing themselves. It is a technique which is often particularly useful in therapeutic situations as the client can continue the therapy in the absence of the therapist. Despite its undoubted usefulness, there is considerable controversy as to the nature of self-hypnosis. Wagstaff (1981) believes that it is possible to explain at least partially self-hypnosis in terms of compliance. Fromm (1975) conducted a study of the similarities and differences between hetero-hypnosis and self-hypnosis, and concluded that more spontaneous imagery was generated in individuals using self-hypnosis. Some individuals reported they reached a deeper level of trance using self-hypnosis, while others reported deeper levels using hetero-hypnosis.

It has also been argued that hetero-hypnosis is really self-hypnosis (Ruch, 1975). Certainly, if hypnosis is a co-operative venture, then perhaps the voice of the hypnotist does not need to be an external one, an internal voice would suffice just as well. Interestingly in this regard one of my subjects reported that when using self-hypnosis the voice he heard internally making suggestions was my voice, not his own. Perhaps the arguments about whether self-hypnosis is a form of hetero-hypnosis or hetero-hypnosis is a form of self-hypnosis are ultimately pointless. It may well be that it is having the suggestions made that is important, not whether they are generated internally or externally.

For those readers who find it difficult to understand how hypnotized subjects can make suggestions to themselves, I suggest they contemplate the following possibilities. The first, rather rigid, possibility is that the subjects have been taught a complete self-hypnotic procedure by the hypnotist. For instance, hypnosis is induced by staring at their thumbnail and repeating over and over to themselves a particular phrase the hypnotist has used to induce hypnosis. Once this has occurred, a number of well-learnt suggestions are automatically triggered, followed finally by the awakening procedure. Another possibility is that the training may make it possible to take into account variation in response to the suggestions, e.g. a certain level of muscular tension acts as a cue to trigger a suggestion, whereas if the tension is below a certain level the cue is different and a different suggestion is triggered.

Many subjects however report that they can control and generate their own suggestions without relying at all on the sort of automatic procedure outlined above. All that is required is the ability to direct one's thoughts for a small percentage of the time for which the session of self-hypnosis lasts. In my experience the majority of hypnotized subjects report that while they are carrying out a suggestion, e.g. directed imagery, they are still able to cough, move their hands etc., and also reflect on the quality of the imagery, worry about their seeming inability to maintain their total attention on the imagery, and fill in the gaps in the scene which the hypnotist is rather vague about. Given that subjects can do these things, I do not find it surprising that subjects can also hypnotize themselves, give themselves suggestions which they respond to appropriately, and awaken themselves.

The technique I prefer to teach to individuals who wish to learn self-hypnosis is a modification of the clenched fist technique (Stein, 1963). I usually commence by inducing hypnosis using a variation of the relaxation method. In this variation I suggest that the relaxation is spreading upwards from the feet, and that as each part of the body relaxes, so all the tension is transferred to the left hand, or whichever is the non-preferred. This hand becomes more and more tightly closed, until eventually the whole of the body is relaxed, apart from the hand, which is by now a tightly clenched fist. I then suggest that the tension flows out of it, and the person enters a deep trance.

I have found that with practice subjects can learn to perform this method of induction in a few seconds. Many of them describe the feeling as like a wave of relaxation spreading along their bodies. Once self-hypnosis has been induced, then the suggestions can be made by the subjects, so there is no need for any other suggestion for clients who become tense in particular situations (except awakening). In addition the method is quite unobtrusive, so can be used by people in quite public situations.

PERSONAL REFLECTIONS

It should be quite clear from the above discussion that there is no one preferred method for either self- or hetero-hypnosis. Instead there are an infinite number of variations of a large number of different techniques. Ideally, hypnotists should use the technique which they believe best suits their particular subject. In practice, however, many hypnotists have their own preferred induction techniques, and often feel unhappy with particular types of induction procedures. For instance, hypnotists with a generally permissive type of approach tend to feel unhappy with authoritarian induction procedures, and vice versa.

Unfortunately, it sometimes happens that an induction procedure does not work. I believe it is important to provide an explanation for this failure which does not require the subject to take the blame. Before the induction commences I will have already pointed out to the subject the co-operative

nature of hypnosis, so I can blame myself for the
failure. Hopefully this will only happen very
occasionally. When the induction technique looks as
if it is not working, it is often possible to switch
to another induction procedure, although care must
be taken to ensure that the subjects do not realize
that this switch is happening because the hypnotist
believes that the original induction procedure is
failing.

SELECTED READING

Hartland, J. (1971) <u>Medical</u> <u>and</u> <u>Dental</u> <u>Hypnosis</u>
     (2nd. ed.), Williams and Wilkins, Baltimore
This book provides a number of induction procedures
which provide a good starting point for hypnotists
wishing to develop their own procedures.

Udolf, R. (1981) <u>Handbook</u> <u>of</u> <u>Hypnosis</u> <u>for</u>
     <u>Professionals</u>, Van Nostrand Reinhold Co., New
     York
There is a very thorough discussion of hypnotic
techniques in chapter three, and also a discussion
of self-hypnosis in chapter six.

Chapter Six

PHENOMENA REPORTED UNDER HYPNOSIS

There are a large number of different phenomena which have been reported under hypnosis. Sometimes these are quite extraordinary, e.g. increased strength; other times they are quite mundane, e.g. relaxation. One aspect of these phenomena which is particularly interesting is the extent to which they occur spontaneously during hypnosis, rather than in response to specific suggestions. There are also some claims for quite dramatic events occurring under hypnosis, e.g. extrasensory perception and memory of past lives. Two separate but related issues are important here. The first is the extent to which these phenomena take place during hypnosis, if at all, and the second is the extent to which they take place only during hypnosis, and not at any other time. Clearly, if some phenomena manifest themselves only during hypnosis, then this would be a means of distinguishing this from other similar states, and from faking.

HALLUCINATIONS

One set of phenomena which has been consistently claimed to occur under hypnosis involves hallucinations, and indeed many susceptibility tests include suggestions for hallucinations. However, I am not convinced that the term 'hallucination' is always being applied in the correct way. I believe that genuine hallucinations have two qualities. One is that they are perceptions which occur in the absence of any real external stimulus. The second is that the person experiencing the hallucinations believes them to be real.
    If this two-fold definition of an hallucination is taken, then probably very few hallucinations

result during hypnosis. When it is suggested that subjects can hear the waves breaking on the shore, how many believe what they imagine they hear to be the result of a real perception? Is the sea really lapping round their ankles, like some modern Canute? No doubt some readers will disagree with my definition of hallucinations and argue that the mere hearing of the sound, seeing of the image is sufficient. This is quite nonsensical. I can sit here now, and play through an image in my mind of Walter Perry scoring a touchdown for the Chicago Bears in the 1986 Superbowl. So too can half the population of the United States. But this is not an hallucination.

Perhaps rather than talking about hallucinations it would be better to examine the vividness of the suggested image. However, some people are capable of extremely vivid imagery in one or more modalities, while others report no imagery at all in some modalities, e.g. olfactory. As someone with vivid visual imagery, I am far from happy if people try to argue that my vivid imagery is really an hallucination. There have been many experiments which have investigated the production of hallucinations during hypnosis, and many of these are reviewed by Udolf (1981). His conclusion is that hallucinations are difficult to elicit under hypnosis. However, it may be that experimental designs even more ingenious than those used so far may be able to demonstrate unequivocally that hallucinations can be produced under hypnosis.

The one piece of evidence which makes me believe that there is a chance that hypnosis may produce genuine hallucinations comes from the verbal reports of subjects, including some of my own. Typically they refer to an experience as being very 'real'. When asked how they knew it was not real, they reply, "because you suggested it".

In other words, although the image seems as vivid as one resulting from a perception of a real object, the subjects know why they are experiencing the image; they were asked to. If an experiment could be set up in which the subjects experienced a suggested image without knowing why, then they may believe it to be real, and hence a genuine hallucination.

As well as positive hallucinations, negative hallucinations have also been claimed to occur during hypnosis. This may be a negative hallucination for the whole of one modality, as in an experiment by Erickson (1938), in which he claimed that some subjects were unable to hear. In other experiments it is suggested to subjects that just a part of their perception is impaired, e.g. Erickson (1939) claimed to induce colour-blindness in deeply hypnotized subjects.

Again, it seems that the evidence for negative hallucinations is far from confirmatory. Although subjects may report negative hallucinations, their responses do not always bear this out. In an experiment by Underwood (1960), subjects reported not being able to see a pattern of lines, but they also reported that another object was distorted in a way possible only if they had perceived the pattern of lines. However, just as hysterical blindness is different from real blindness, suggested blindness may be different too.

It may be that thinking about suggested alterations in perception as hallucinations is inappropriate. Hallucinations have particular properties which it seems that many researchers have put to one side. Rather than talking about hallucinations in the context of hypnosis, it might well prove less confusing simply to talk about alterations in perception.

TRANCE LOGIC

One of the most interesting of all apparent hypnotic phenomena is trance logic, a term first used by Orne (1959). The essence of trance logic is that the hypnotized person appears to be able to believe simultaneously ideas or perceptions which are incompatible, and to be unaware of their incompatibility. Orne (1962) reported that if hypnotized subjects are instructed to negatively hallucinate a chair (imagine that it is no longer there), then when instructed also to walk round the room with their eyes open they refrain from bumping into the chair, while maintaining that they are unable to see the chair. Simulating subjects however, bump into the chair (Bowers, 1976). It is not always clear in these sort of experiments whether hypnotized subjects actually believe that the chair no longer exists, or that it still exists but they are no longer able to perceive its existence. If it is the latter, then it is not illogical to claim they cannot see the chair but avoid walking into it, since one would expect the subjects to have a memory of the chair's location. Moving the chair to another position provides a much better test, since if hypnotized subjects claiming they are unable to perceive the chair do not bump into it, this demonstrates much more clearly the incompatibility of their responses, as they cannot be relying on memory to know where the chair is.

A similar kind of trance logic has been claimed for hallucinations of 'doubles'. Here hypnotized subjects are requested to hallucinate an object which is already present in the room, or perhaps required to hallucinate a person who then walks into the room. McDonald and Smith (1975), Sheehan, Obstoj and McConkey (1976), and Sheehan (1977) found however that not all hypnotized subjects reported seeing these 'double' hallucinations, while a number of simulating subjects also reported seeing them. Quite where the incompatibility lies in this example is debatable. What seems to have a considerable bearing on the matter is the extent to which subjects believe that the object they are hallucinating really exists as opposed to being simply a product of their imagination. If the subject really believes the hallucinated object exists, then it might be incompatible to see more than one, although even in this case some rational explanation could be found for their dual existence. However, if the subjects know that one of the objects they are seeing is an hallucination, and the real object then appears, then I contend there is nothing incompatible in this, for it would be equivalent to expecting an hallucination to disappear when informed that it was an hallucination.

Another type of trance logic involves transparent hallucinations. Here hypnotized subjects report being able to see a real object 'through' the hallucinated object (Johnson, Maher and Barber, 1972; Sheehan et al., 1976). Again, some simulators also report this phenomenon. Clearly it is illogical to see something when it should be totally obscured by another object. Despite this, if the subjects believe that what they are seeing is an hallucination rather than a real object, it may not be illogical at all. There are few rules to which hallucinations have to adhere, and it may well be that for many subjects one of the imagined properties of hallucinations is that it is possible to see through them.

Trance logic is an elusive phenomenon. Although it has been claimed to exist, the more closely it is examined, the more difficult it is to pin down. Due mainly to problems of not knowing whether subjects

really believe an object is real or is just an
hallucination, or really does not exist or is a
negative hallucination, it is possible to
demonstrate that the claimed illogicality may not
exist. Nevertheless, trance logic remains a
fascinating area within hypnosis, and it is to be
hoped that further experiments clarify the issues
raised here by investigating subjects' beliefs,
perhaps by adopting similar methods to Sheehan and
McConkey (1982).

TIME DISTORTION

McCue (1982) identifies two types of time distortion
which have been alleged to occur during hypnosis,
time expansion, where relatively short periods of
time are experienced as if they were much longer,
and time condensation, where a relatively long
period of time has been experienced as if it were
much shorter. He also makes the point that our
perception of duration is determined by our
activities; generally boring tasks seem to take
longer than interesting tasks. Ornstein (1970)
discusses some possible reasons for this. One
explanation is that time duration is judged by the
number of events (or targets) experienced. Looking
back over a particular time period, the more events
which have been focused on, the longer the period is
likely to have been perceived to be.
    It is important here to draw a distinction
between process and duration (Piaget, 1971). Process
relates to our experience of the passing of time as
it is happening, and the more events which are
occurring, the faster time seems to pass. Duration
refers to how long a time period is judged to be
looking back from the present to a particular event,
e.g. from now to your last meal, and the more events
which have occurred in this period, the longer it
will be perceived to be. At first there might appear
to be a contradiction here concerning time
perception from the point of view of process and
duration. This apparent contradiction can be
resolved by hypothesizing that time is judged by the
number of events occurring. On a moment-to-moment
basis (process), if nothing much is happening, then
time is perceived as passing slowly. Looking back to
a particular event (duration) if not much has
happened, then the time interval is judged to be
fairly short. It is almost as if events were
considered to be equivalent to a particular time

interval, so that if events occur in quick succession time appears to be passing quickly, while looking back to a particular event the duration from that event to the present is judged by the number of events occurring.

There is no doubt that this is an over-simplification of events, e.g. it is likely that certain events are judged as taking longer than others. Despite this the hypothesis has a certain explanatory power, and as has been shown, it is possible to apply similar analyses to time distortion under hypnosis (McCue, 1982).

Bowers (1979), Bowers and Brenneman (1979), and St. Jean, MacLeod, Coe and Howard (1982) have shown that subjects typically underestimate time intervals under hypnosis. Bowers (1979) and Bowers and Brenneman (1979) proposed that this was due to the subjects' absorption and imaginative involvement in the proceedings. St. Jean et al. (1982), following Ornstein's reasoning (1969), tested the hypothesis that underestimation of time duration occurs to the extent that subjects are amnesic for the events in a hypnotic session. However, no such relationship was found. Despite this, the results of the experiment do not preclude an explanation of hypnotic time distortion based on the number of events occurring. It is possible that the number of events in a hypnotic session may be much less than in most other situations subjects experience, causing them to underestimate the duration. There is really nothing incompatible in subjects being imaginatively involved and experiencing relatively few events.

There have also been attempts to alter subjects' perception of time duration by hypnotic suggestions (Cooper and Erickson, 1959). When it was suggested to the subjects that time would go slowly, and minutes would seem like hours, this was the experience which many subjects reported. In addition, this expanded time was filled with imagined events, like watching an entire football match in a few minutes. It may be possible to argue that subjects have not actually imagined watching a whole match, but only certain parts of it, i.e. the times when the ball is in play. However, when a subject maintains that she has counted over one thousand items in ten seconds (Cooper and Erickson, 1950), such explanations cannot apply. McCue (1982) suggests that this may be due to the activation of memories in parallel rather than in series, so that many more could be recalled in a short space of time than would otherwise be possible. The subject remains unaware of this parallel recall process and believing that the memories have been accessed serially reports that the session lasted for much longer than it actually did.

If the subjects are experiencing relatively short periods of time as being much longer than they really are, then the possibility arises that they may be able to perform particular tasks which would normally take longer than the time period they have available. One method which attempts to test this hypothesis involves subjects learning material and then measures the amount of learning by using a free recall task. If subjects are hypnotized for a particular length of time, which they are then told will seem much longer, then it may be the case that they will be able to learn more than a control group who are not told that time will seem much longer. A number of experiments have, with slightly different experimental designs, tested this hypothesis.

Barber and Calverley (1964) found no such differences in performance on the learning task. Krauss, Katzell and Krauss (1974) found that subjects told three minutes would seem like ten, apparently learnt as much in the three minutes as a control group learnt in ten. Johnson (1976) and Wagstaff and Ovenden (1979) failed to replicate these results, so even if subjects can experience a minute as seeming to last for an hour, it is not clear that they can use the time as if it were sixty minutes rather than just one.

Given that the normal state of affairs is for subjects to underestimate the duration of a hypnotic session it is surprising that there seems to be nothing other than anecdotal reports (Cooper and Erickson, 1959) concerning the extent to which the passage of time can be speeded up. Clearly, if this phenomenon can be reliably induced, then it may well have clinical significance, particularly in the relief of pain.

Time distortion is a fascinating area, one in which subjects' experiences seem to undergo quite dramatic changes, but a definitive explanation for these changes is still awaited. It also remains to be seen whether these experiential changes can be utilized by subjects in some practical fashion, e.g. to learn more quickly or to make painful events seem of much shorter duration.

IMAGERY

Part of the 'folklore' of hypnosis is that imagery
is enhanced during hypnosis, specifically that it is
more vivid, more effort-free, and richer. However,
although there have been some studies which support
this belief (Schofield and Platoni, 1976; Starker,
1974), other studies such as that by Barber and
Wilson (1977) do not support this view. There are
several factors which may help account for these
contradictory findings.

One is that many of the studies used self-
report scales for measuring imagery, which may not
be ideal in these circumstances, since they have a
narrow coverage (typically some aspects of visual
imagery). Another factor is that the essentially
subjective nature of imagery makes it particularly
difficult to measure by any means. It is also
difficult to be sure what subjects mean when they
say their imagery is 'more vivid'. Perhaps in fact
they are just concentrating on it more, which has
the effect of making it seem more vivid.

There is also some evidence that eidetic
imagery may be produced in a few extremely good
hypnotic subjects (Wallace, 1978). It appears that
these subjects had possessed eidetic imagery as
children, and in some way the hypnosis brought this
ability back to them. These findings are rather
controversial, and an attempt at replication by
Spanos, Ansari and Stam (1979) was unsuccessful.

AGE REGRESSION

Age regression is an extremely interesting
phenomenon in which subjects are taken back to an
earlier period in their life. One way of doing this
is to suggest that subjects count back from their
present age one year at a time, until they reach the
desired age. Another technique is to ask them to
imagine a particular event, such as a birthday. When
they are imagining this it is suggested that they
are really the age they were at this remembered
event.

It is interesting to speculate as to whether
age regressed persons genuinely believe that they
are this age or whether they are in some sense
pretending. This does not imply that they are
deliberately trying to fool the experimenter.
However it is very often not clear to subjects how
they are supposed to react. Are they supposed to

believe they are really age regressed, and have no knowledge of events which have taken place since this time, or are they supposed to act, as best they can, as if they are really that particular age, while still being aware that they are not?

Even if subjects really believe that they are regressed to a particular age, another difficulty remains. This is the age appropriateness of the subjects' responses, for instance, is drawing produced during age regression really like that of a person of that age? Many studies have attempted to answer this question.

An experiment by Orne (1951) investigated the age appropriateness of subjects' responses when they had been regressed to the age of six. Although there was no doubt that the subjects' drawing and writing was more childlike, as was also found by Fellows and Creamer (1978), there were several incongruities. One was the subjects' ability to understand difficult words, and to be able to spell them. The subjects' drawing and writing also showed both adult and child-like characteristics. Perry and Walsh (1978) concluded that subjects who are age regressed to a particular age do not suffer total amnesia for everything they have learnt since that age.

It appears then that the subjects' response is not always age appropriate, and many studies attest to this. Barber (1962) reviewed studies which used intelligence tests to investigate how age appropriate subjects' responses were. The general conclusion is that when subjects are age regressed their scores are more immature than when they are not age regressed. However, their scores are still not really age appropriate; usually the scores are more like that of a more mature child. Thus, in Brenneman's (1978) terms, reinstatement, which is a return to more childlike modes of cognitive and emotional functioning, is a more apt description for what is generally observed than ablation, which is the functional loss of all the subject's knowledge, abilities, and memories acquired after the suggested age.

Age regression is a particularly impressive phenomenon, even if there are some anomalies in the age regressed subjects' behaviours. However, an even more impressive phenomenon is age progression. Here it is suggested that the subject is progressing forwards in time. This can be suggested in a variety of ways, for instance by counting forward from the present year or by increasing the subject's age.

Typically, subjects can give accounts of things

which have not yet happened. However, clearly they
do not really 'know' these things, but are
extrapolating them from their current knowledge.
There may also be a degree of wish fulfilment
present, for instance a subject may say he is
married to a woman who in reality he knows he will
never marry. It is possible to use age progression
to assist in therapy, by suggesting that the client
goes forward to a time when the problem no longer
exists. This can be useful for people with long-
standing problems who cannot remember (or never
knew) what it is like to be without the problem.

Both age regression and age progression are
fascinating phenomena, which can be seen from the
amount of research which has been carried out in
these areas. It also illustrates well the difficulty
in deciding whether subjects are: faking (simulating
the behaviour in an attempt to deceive the
experimenter), simulating (performing the behaviour
because that is what they have been requested to
do, but without being hypnotized), being genuine
(performing the behaviour under hypnosis).

These three methods of responding are very
difficult to investigate, because the distinctions
between them are not always clear. Faking is very
hard to distinguish from being genuine, as is
simulating. It may be argued that simulating should
be easy to distinguish from being genuine, but this
is not necessarily the case, because it is possible
that some of the subjects in the simulating group
may actually be hypnotized. To ensure that the
simulating group is as similar as possible to the
group receiving the hypnotic induction, they often
receive task motivational instructions, which may
actually induce hypnosis in some subjects.

MEMORY ENHANCEMENT

Over recent years there has been much debate
concerning the role of hypnosis in memory and
learning, specifically, whether or not hypnosis can
enhance learning and memory, a phenomenon often
known as hypermnesia. In psychology there is a huge
literature on memory and learning, in part because
there are so many variables which can be controlled
by a variety of experimental designs, giving rise to
a large number of different experiments. One of the
most important of these variables is the
meaningfulness of the material. Dhanens and Lundy
(1975) found that hypnosis had no effect on recall

of nonsense syllables, but the group who received hypnosis plus task motivating instructions showed enhanced recall, although it must be noted that there has been some criticism of this experiment (Smith, 1983).

However, Cooper and London (1973) found no enhancement of memory for hypnotized subjects in recall of a scientific article, although it may be argued that this material may not be particularly meaningful to some subjects! Perhaps in the enhancement of memory recall using hypnosis it is the emotional content of the material which is most crucial. Certainly this appears to be the case in clinical studies which seem to indicate the usefulness of hypnosis in uncovering memories of repressed events. If this was the only way in which hypnosis could aid recall then its uses in memory enhancement would be rather limited.

Wagstaff (1984) concludes that hypnosis does not appear to aid recall of nonsense syllables, but that the evidence for meaningful material is inconclusive. This has considerable implications for using hypnosis in areas such as forensic medicine to aid witness recall, which will be discussed in a later chapter.

Another claim for memory enhancement during hypnosis involves revivification, a condition in which a subject gains access to memories from childhood that cannot be recalled in the normal state. Age regression is usually used to bring about revivification. Although there is some evidence (Reiff and Scheerer, 1959) that subjects can recall accurately early memories, it is also the case that given strategies to help them, subjects can do this without hypnosis.

Readers may wish to try this themselves. Simply think back to an event in childhood you can remember. Then think of what you were doing just before this event, and just after. Use visual and auditory imagery to help you. Next, try to isolate some event related to this period that you do not remember thinking about for a long time. You may well be surprised at how many memories return as a result of this simple strategy.

Revivification seems to consist of recall of a number of memories, but any 'gaps' appear to be filled in using knowledge drawn not from direct memories, but from other sources. These include what others have told the subjects about this period in their lives, and inferences drawn from the knowledge they do possess.

MEMORY FOR PAST LIVES

In the popular press there are occasional reports of individuals who are hypnotized and are then able to recall details from past lives. This raises several interesting issues. One of these is the extent to which this is actually possible. Most serious researchers in the area of hypnotic phenomena would be extremely surprised if this was truly happening. The idea of reincarnation is one which scientists in general find hard to accept, and acceptance of this idea is of course necessary if we are going to accept that people can 'remember' past lives under hypnosis.

However, it is also true that many people who apparently 'recall' past lives do actually believe that they lived them. How might this be explained? One possible explanation is that the individuals who are able to recall past lives are extremely susceptible. The hypnotist suggests that they are able to recall a past life, and they concur with the suggestion. Not only do they construct a past life on request, they then believe they really lived it.

It is often reported that the details the people provide cannot possibly have been known to them unless they really did live in that particular time as that particular individual. There have also been some attempts to verify information which subjects have given. However, it must be remembered that the fact that people are able to recall a mass of knowledge which they were apparently not conscious of before the hypnotic session does not prove that they gained this information as a result of living a past life. It is far more likely that this represents information which they had available to them all the time, but which they had simply not thought about for a long period of time.

Nor is it really necessary to argue that it is the hypnosis which has been directly responsible for the recall of this information. It is really far more likely that it is the amount of time and questioning which is responsible for the individuals being able to recall this information. I suspect that the role of hypnosis is much more likely to be in convincing very susceptible subjects that they really did live a past life.

Once this belief is established, it provides a framework on which they can append genuine and fabricated memories. It is almost certainly the case that some of the information given is accurate, except in the sense that it is a not real memory of the person concerned but was acquired from books, television, etc. The rest of the material probably results from fabrication, in the same fashion as much of the information which is recalled in witnesses who have been hypnotized is fabricated.

AMNESIA

Amnesia may occur as the result of direct suggestion, or it may occur spontaneously. Although spontaneous post-hypnotic amnesia is often thought of as a sign of the subject being in a deep trance, it is a very elusive phenomenon in experimental settings. One problem is in defining spontaneous amnesia. If it is argued that it is forgetting of all or nearly all of what happened when the subject was hypnotized, in the absence of any instruction to do so, then it is necessary to look carefully at the knowledge the subject brings to the situation. If the subject believes prior to the hypnotic session that one of the results of being hypnotized is amnesia, then any amnesia which does result cannot be classed as spontaneous.

An experiment by Young and Cooper (1972) demonstrates this well. Half the subjects heard a lecture in which it was suggested that post-hypnotic amnesia typically occurred, while the other half were informed that amnesia never spontaneously occurred. Significantly more of those told that amnesia occurred spontaneously showed it. It may be sensible to look at the type of information which is forgotten, and the type which is typically recalled in attempting to understand the disparity between clinical and experimental studies. The material which seems to be forgotten after clinical sessions is often more affect laden, and may well have been repressed prior to the hypnotic session. It is perhaps not so surprising that this material is forgotten.

As is the case with many aspects of hypnosis, post-hypnotic amnesia is a complex phenomenon. Many writers have described post-hypnotic amnesia as simply the result of subjects being told under hypnosis that they would forget all or part of what occurred during the hypnotic session. They are often also told that they will be able to recall this 'forgotten' material when a particular cue ('release' word) is given. However, this is really an over-simplification, and there are many factors which need to be considered.

One is the extent to which subjects may use particular strategies to prevent themselves remembering the material, such as thinking about something else. This is perhaps rather similar to directed forgetting, in which subjects typically learn some new information, and then receive instructions to forget some or all of it (Epstein, 1972). As Wagstaff (1981) concludes, it seems difficult to argue that subjects who cannot recall something because they are simply not thinking about it have actually forgotten the material.

One distinction which is often made in post-hypnotic amnesia is between source and content amnesia. Source amnesia occurs when subjects are able to recall the information they were given during the hypnotic session, but are unable to remember its source, i.e. where they learnt it. In content amnesia the information itself cannot be recalled.

There seem to be some obvious similarities here to the distinction made by Tulving (1972) between semantic and episodic memory. Briefly, semantic memory consists of general knowledge, such as the capital of England, while episodic memory consists of more personal information, such as what a person had for breakfast. The similarity lies in the fact that there is generally supposed to be no memory for the source of information in semantic memory, although there may be a corresponding entry in episodic memory detailing the situation in which the information was learnt.

If one believes in this dichotomy, it is interesting to speculate as to whether some information learnt during hypnosis may be stored in semantic memory only, and have no entry in episodic memory at all. If this were so, then the term 'source amnesia' is rather misleading, for it would be more accurate to say that the source of the material had never been learnt.

Udolf (1981) comments that source amnesia usually occurs spontaneously, and is not often suggested under hypnosis. Wagstaff (1981) has argued that source amnesia is not limited to hypnotic subjects, but also occurs in simulating subjects. Without further evidence, it seems difficult to argue that source amnesia is any different from simply forgetting where one heard something. Anyone sitting through a number of papers at a conference may well forget in which presentation a particular point was made.

Post-hypnotic amnesia seems to be an elusive

phenomenon. Despite the ease with which it can apparently be induced, there is no accepted explanation for why it occurs. Indeed, it is not always clear that post-hypnotic amnesia is really any different from amnesia which may be produced in a group of simulators.

What appears to be often overlooked is that subjects are not passive individuals in the hypnotic session. They do not generally respond to the hypnotist's suggestions without any conscious thought. If subjects are requested to forget some or all of what takes place during the hypnotic session, what are they to do? What is hard to believe is that they automatically forget the information, just by willing it. Anyone who has ever tried to forget something will know how hard it is. What seems much more likely is that subjects instructed to forget adopt one of a number of strategies, such as refusing to think about the material, perhaps distracting themselves by thinking about something else.

It is to be hoped that future research will emphasize the active nature of subjects during hypnosis. Subjects bring all their knowledge and strategies to the session, and any theory of post-hypnotic amnesia must take this into account. The theory which seems best able to account for post-hypnotic amnesia, and for that matter amnesia in simulators, is strategic enactment (Spanos and Radtke, 1982). Subjects being tested for amnesia consistently disattend from the retrieval cues provided for the target material, until they are given the release cue. They then attend to the retrieval cues, and hence recall the material they were previously unable to recall.

Another strategy which subjects may use, although it is not reported by Spanos and Radtke (1982) is to use the retrieval cues to retrieve material other than the target material. Whatever the retrieval cues are, instead of using them as a strategy to aid recall of the target material the subject can use them in other ways, perhaps attempting to think of the opposite meaning of the words used in the retrieval strategy, perhaps of words which rhyme with them. It can be argued that this is a deliberate attempt not to think of the material, and hence cannot account for subjects who say they are genuinely unable to remember the material, but it seems to me that, given the role the unconscious plays in the storage of memories and their structure, it would·be churlish to insist that it might not also have a part in deciding what to let through into the conscious mind, what to not let through, and what strategies to use to assist in this regard. Anyone who has ever experienced the tip-of-the-tongue phenomenon has some insight into the apparent failure of normal retrieval strategies.

ANIMAL HYPNOSIS

Animal hypnosis is the term which has been traditionally used to refer to the finding that many animals, when they are held in such a way that they are unable to move, enter a state in which they apparently cannot move when the restraint is removed. This can last for quite some time. It has been argued that this condition may also be brought about by a sudden shock.

It seems apparent that the phenomenon is really misnamed. The animal is not hypnotized in the sense in which most researchers believe hypnosis takes place; tonic immobility is the term which is often used to describe the near catatonic state which results. However, as Gibson (1977) argues, it may be that some humans who are supposedly hypnotized are really in a state of tonic immobility.

It is possible, according to Gibson (1977), that some patients who have been operated on may not really have been hypnotized, but that the prospect of being operated on was enough to induce a state of tonic immobility. Whether they felt the pain of the operation or were simply unable to move is a matter to reflect on.

PERSONAL REFLECTIONS

I hope that readers who puzzled over the title of this chapter 'Phenomena Reported Under Hypnosis' may have some idea of why I chose such a title. It seems to me that although many phenomena have been reported under hypnosis, sometimes there is little experimental evidence to back up these reports, while the phenomena which do occur under hypnosis seem to occur just as easily in simulating subjects.

Human beings have a vast repertoire of behaviour, and can often find some strategy which enables them to carry out the most bizarre suggestions. Throughout its history hypnosis has been seen as a state in which the investigator has freedom to suggest all manner of strange activities.

When subjects have acted on these suggestions the temptation has been to ascribe this behaviour to the peculiarity of hypnosis. However, as experimenters have become more critical, and used simulating subjects as controls, they have found that the majority of these strange behaviours can also occur in subjects who are not hypnotized.

There may be some differences between simulators and hypnotized subjects, but at the moment such differences appear slight. Generally, subjects instructed to simulate and given task motivational instructions show no differences in their responses from hypnotized subjects. Individual differences seem much more important in determining to what extent subjects will respond, irrespective of what group they are in.

To finish on a positive note, the more that various hypnotic phenomena can be investigated and explained, the more likely it is that the nature of hypnosis will be resolved.

SELECTED READING

Spanos, N. P. and Radtke, H. L. (1982) 'Hypnotic Amnesia as Strategic Enactment: A Cognitive, Social-Psychological Perspective', <u>Research Communications</u> in <u>Psychology, Psychiatry and Behavior</u>, <u>7</u>, 215-31
This provides a detailed examination of hypnotic amnesia, with an interpretation based on the strategic enactment approach. Although it relates to only one of the areas covered in this chapter, it is well worth reading for the beautiful way in which the authors reinterpret amnesia in terms of strategic enactment.

Udolf, R. (1981) <u>Handbook of Hypnosis for Professionals</u>, Van Nostrand Reinhold Company, New York
This book contains a very detailed review of many hypnotic phenomena. Udolf has delved deeply into the experimental literature, and surfaced with some excellent critiques.

Wagstaff, G. F. (1981) <u>Hypnosis, Compliance and Belief</u>, The Harvester Press, Brighton
Wagstaff examines very critically a number of hypnotic phenomena, and perhaps not surprisingly decides that compliance and belief almost always offer satisfactory alternative explanations. The

style   in which this is done,   however,   makes it   a
very interesting passage to read.

Chapter Seven

THERAPEUTIC USES OF HYPNOSIS

Over the years hypnosis has been used in a wide variety of clinical situations. However, despite this there are relatively few conclusions which can be drawn concerning its effectiveness (Wadden and Anderton, 1982). Judging the effectiveness of any form of therapy is notoriously difficult, and this is particularly true of hypnosis. Perhaps the greatest difficulty is that hypnosis is nearly always used in conjunction with other therapeutic approaches.

There are several ways of examining and determining therapeutic effectiveness, employing a range of methodological techniques, e.g. meta-analysis (Smith, Glass and Miller, 1980). Oatley (1984) has argued that many non-directive therapists believe that the question of whether therapy is effective or not is meaningless. They consider that many aspects of the therapeutic relationship are essentially immeasurable, and one may as well attempt to measure the benefits of friendship, or love. This is not to deny that there are benefits, but rather to argue that the benefits probably lie in areas which are practically impossible to measure.

This in turn throws up a new problem, for if a therapy is shown to be producing no measurable benefits, then proponents of that particular therapy can claim that the benefits are simply not measurable ones. Opponents of the therapy can argue that there is no basis for believing that it has any benefits. There is no easy answer to this dilemma. The particular theoretical stances of the therapists determines their views as to whether or not therapy can be measured. Precisely the same perspective can be taken when examining the effectiveness of therapeutic approaches involving hypnosis.

It seems particularly important to make use of

published studies of the effectiveness of therapeutic approaches involving hypnosis, where traditionally much of the reporting seems to have been anecdotal. However, this should not be taken as implying that I have no sympathy for those who claim that the benefits of therapy may not be measurable. In certain areas this may well be a viable argument, but in other areas it would seem that the benefits should be directly measurable, and indeed recent research often makes strenuous attempts to measure the effectiveness of the procedures used.

As mentioned previously, there is another problem when discussing the effectiveness of hypnosis, which arises because hypnosis is usually regarded as an adjunct to therapy, rather than a therapy in its own right. Hence the discussion of therapeutic uses of hypnosis is not simply a matter of cataloguing various areas in which hypnosis has been employed. Instead it is also necessary to consider the various types of therapy which are typically used during hypnosis. The first part of this chapter examines a number of therapies which can be used in conjunction with hypnosis. Although I have placed the therapies under various categories, I fully realize that the categories are not mutually exclusive, and some therapies, perhaps most, do not fit easily under any one heading. I am also aware that there are many which are not here. I will return to these omissions later in the chapter.

HYPNOSIS AS THERAPY

This deliberately provocative title should not be taken as meaning that I believe wholeheartedly that hypnosis itself is a form of therapy. On the other hand I do not believe that the possibility should be dismissed as readily as some authors suggest (Frischholz and Spiegel, 1983; McCue, 1983). In a stimulating article entitled 'Hypnosis Is Not Therapy' Frischholz and Spiegel argue that many writers seem to believe that hypnosis is a form of therapy in itself. Furthermore they believe that the term "hypnotherapy" is a misnomer, since it implies exactly that. Gibson (1983) is in agreement with this. He states that:

'I agree with the authors that the term "hypnotherapy" is regrettable (whether it is used by Harley Street clinicians or by the quacks who advertise in the windows of

stationers' shops) because the term
implies that hypnosis of itself has a
therapeutic value' (Gibson, 1983, p. 9).'

There are at least two interesting points here. One
is that hypnotherapy is used in quite a different
way from the way it is used in the title of this
book. My use of the term is in reference to any
therapeutic situation in which hypnosis is used,
whereas in the articles mentioned above, the
range of application seems to be much wider. Leaving
this semantic ambiguity aside, the problem still
remains as to whether hypnosis itself can be a form
of therapy.
    One way to approach this question is to examine
typical phenomena which occur during hypnosis
spontaneously. However, as the reader should by now
be aware, such a wide variety of phenomena may occur
that it is difficult to state categorically which
are 'typical'. These phenomena depend on the
expectations of the subjects, their susceptibility,
and the induction procedure used (if any). Many
subjects, depending on the induction procedure used,
experience feelings of relaxation, and report
afterwards that they feel a lack of tension, and
that minor headaches, and other aches and pains,
disappear.
    Certainly I would not wish to argue that
hypnosis is a 'general' form of therapy. On the
other hand it seems strange to deny the comments and
observations of many individuals who claim that they
feel 'better' after being hypnotized, even those who
are hypnotized for experiments and demonstrations
rather than for therapeutic purposes. I am not
claiming that anyone is 'cured', whatever that might
mean, by just being hypnotized, but I am certain
that many clients do experience a feeling of
increased physical and mental well-being.

HYPNOSIS AND ANALYTIC PSYCHOTHERAPY

Hypnosis may be used as an aid in analytic
psychotherapy. As Udolf (1981) states, the aims are
to find out the meaning the symptoms have for the
client, and to bring about a resolution of the
unconscious conflicts which are responsible for the
symptoms. It is important to emphasize that many
hypnotic phenomena may be employed to realize the
aims, but however hypnosis is used it is subservient
to those aims. In other words, the analytic

psychotherapist draws on hypnosis to help the analysis, just as any other technique may be used if the analyst thinks it appropriate.

One of the hypnotic techniques which may be used is age regression, which might serve a number of purposes during the analysis. An obvious use is to help recover an early or even repressed memory. A good example of this is given by French (1984, pp. 99-104), who describes how an unpleasant sexual experience as a boy resulted in the development of a severe stutter. According to French, uncovering this memory using hypnosis led to a cessation of the stammer. Similar examples can be found in abundance.

Another reason for using age regression is that it may enable the client to return to an earlier mode of thinking, for example primary process, which according to Freudian psychoanalysts is characterized by imagery. This may allow the client to achieve new insights by forcing a re-conceptualization of the problem(s) and the surrounding events. Age regression also allows the client to return to a time before the onset of the symptoms. This can often give the analyst valuable information concerning the emotional state of the client prior to the development of the symptoms.

The analyst may also make use of guided imagery to explore certain areas with the client, and bring about new understanding. This is a technique in which the analyst can ask the client to imaginally represent certain situations and explore by suggestion real or potential outcomes of those situations.

One interesting technique is to make use of hypnotically induced dreams. The exploration of dreams and their interpretation is perhaps the best known analytic technique, and has certainly had a long history within analysis. By inducing dreams hypnotically, the analyst has some control over the content of the dream. For instance, the analyst could instruct the client to dream about becoming lost in a wood, and then later find out from the client how that dream progressed, and what the emotional reaction was. This is potentially a very powerful technique, since the analyst can in a sense 'check out' the insights gained in previous therapeutic sessions.

There are so many possible uses of hypnosis in analysis that it is potentially one of the most valuable tools available. An experienced analyst can use hypnosis in an extremely creative fashion, bringing into play a whole range of phenomena which occur most readily under hypnosis. However, the analyst must not forget that hypnosis is not analysis, but only a means of aiding analysis.

BEHAVIOUR THERAPY

Behaviour therapy is a generic term used to cover a number of different types of therapy. However, these different types of therapy all have their roots in learning theory, and mostly draw heavily on operant conditioning techniques.

Behaviour therapists tend to concentrate on the symptoms which the client presents, and are much less concerned with the underlying 'cause' of the symptom. Indeed, many behaviour therapists do not believe that symptoms are caused by an underlying illness, but that the symptoms themselves are the illness. These symptoms have been learnt according to behaviourist principles, and since these types of behaviour are maladaptive, behaviourist principles must be used to remove them. More specifically, the symptoms can be removed by using the process of extinction, and new behaviours can be learned in their place.

There is generally no attempt to investigate the causes of the symptoms, nor is there any attempt to investigate the meaning of the symptoms for the client. Furthermore, there is no attempt to change the attitudes and feelings of the client. It is not clear whether behaviour therapists believe these are irrelevant, or whether they believe that removing the symptoms will bring about a corresponding change in the client's belief systems.

The general approach of the behaviour therapist is to take a detailed case history and carry out a functional analysis. From this the therapist can work out what aspects of the behaviour are being controlled by what stimuli. It then becomes a matter of breaking down particular associations and building up new ones, usually by designing a specific treatment regime which is likely to differ from client to client.

Within this general framework there are a number of behaviourist approaches. Although they often seem quite different, they are all based on the same principles. Initially, behaviour therapy and hypnosis may seem strange bedfellows, but as Lazarus (1971) and Weitzenhoffer (1972) claim, hypnosis can be a useful adjunct to therapy. During the following examination of different forms of behaviour therapy the facilitatory effects of hypnosis will be made clear.

Systematic Desensitisation

This is a type of behaviour therapy which is based on the principle of reciprocal inhibition (Wolpe, 1958). According to this, fear and relaxation are incompatible responses and cannot coexist, i.e. a person cannot be both afraid and relaxed at the same time. The task for the therapist is therefore to ensure that the client is in a state of relaxation, and remains so even when the fear evoking stimulus is presented. (It must be noted that there is some disagreement about the precise mechanism by which reciprocal inhibition operates.)

A typical procedure to accomplish this is as follows. The first stage is to work out with the client a hierarchy of fearful stimuli. For instance, in the case of a client with a spider phobia, the client may decide that having a large spider run over his or her hand is the most fear evoking, while looking at a picture of a spider only gives rise to mild fear. In between are other conditions, such as looking at a large spider, looking at a small spider, looking at a web, seeing a spider on television, etc. These can all be rank ordered, and a rating of fearfulness attached to each of them. This rating is often carried out using a scale of subjective unit of disturbance (SUD), which typically varies from 1 to 100, where 0 represents no fear, and 100 represents maximum possible fear.

The next stage is to teach the client a relaxation technique. Once the client can relax, the least fearful stimulus in the hierarchy is introduced. Since relaxation and fear are incompatible, the client should now experience no fear. If some residual fear is reported, then the relaxation procedure must be repeated, until the client's estimation of fear on the SUD scale is 0. When this is successfully accomplished, the therapist can go on to the next stimulus in the hierarchy. This stimulus should now produce rather less fear than it did at first due to the generalization effect, and so the procedure continues until the client reaches the most feared stimulus in the hierarchy and is able to deal with this.

In practice I have found that generalization from one level in the hierarchy to another level is far from complete, particularly as the client gets

closer to the most feared stimulus. One general
strategy is to find out what would satisfy the
client. Going back to the previous example, in my
experience few clients would wish to be able to have
a spider run over their hand. Rather, most would
rather not panic when they see a spider, and many
would like to be able to remove it in some way.
(Interestingly, I have never had a client who
reported they wished to kill a phobic creature). To
be able to remove the phobic object seems to be a
sensible end-point to aim for, and coupled with some
generalization to the stimuli at the top of the
hierarchy, for the vast majority of clients this
represents a satisfactory outcome for the treatment.

Potentially, there are a lot of ways in which
hypnosis can be used within systematic
desensitisation. As mentioned earlier, there is a
great deal of similarity between hypnosis and
relaxation, and the relaxation stage of this
therapeutic procedure is often carried out using
hypnosis. The presentation of the various stimuli in
the hierarchy can be done purely in imagination,
using hypnosis to suggest the stimuli. Dengrove
(1973) states that hypnosis can also be used to
prepare the client for the use of visual imagery,
and that some of the techniques which are available
under hypnosis can be utilized as well. An example
of this would be the use of age regression with a
client who found it very difficult to experience
enough fear imaginally. The client could be taken
back to a situation in which the right level of fear
had been experienced, and this would overcome the
problem.

Hypnosis can no doubt be a very valuable
adjunct to systematic desensitisation. It is clearly
recommended if the client is a reasonable hypnotic
subject, but finds it hard to relax, or hard to
visualize particular stimuli in the hierarchy. If
the client is a poor hypnotic subject then there is
clearly no point in attempting to use hypnosis.
Conversely, if the client is good at both relaxing
and visualizing there is no real reason to use
hypnosis.

Flooding
Flooding is a technique whose main application is in
the treatment of phobias. The client is exposed to
the phobic object in a situation in which there is
no possibility of escape. Consequently a great deal
of fear is aroused, and the client also experiences

the concomitant physiological reactions, such as nausea, increased perspiration, heart rate, breathing, etc. It is crucially important that the client remains in this situation until these physiological changes have returned to normal.

Although there is some doubt about the precise theoretical basis of this treatment, I believe the most likely explanation is as follows. Often people with phobias go to considerable trouble to avoid the phobic object, e.g. a person with a phobia about lifts is unlikely ever to enter one. The implication of this is that the phobia will never be extinguished, for in order for extinction to take place the person must experience the stimulus (phobic object) in the absence of the reinforcement. The reinforcement for a person with a phobia is the relief which comes from escaping the phobic object. In flooding the client is confronted by the fear-evoking stimulus, and is unable to experience the reinforcement normally felt by escaping from the situation, because this is not permitted.

Furthermore, the intense physiological responses to fear cannot be maintained by the body for very long. As the body's physiological state returns to normal, so the feelings of fear recede too. This is only to be expected since the subjective experience of fear is partly dependent on an examination of physiological arousal.

Flooding is well suited to hypnosis, if the client is a good subject. It may well be extremely difficult to set up a suitably fearful situation for the client in real life, and in some cases may even be physically dangerous. Consequently if the client can imagine the situation under hypnosis, then these difficulties are removed. Although the therapist does not know what the client is actually thinking about, if various physiological measures are taken then there is often little doubt that it is something extremely fear-evoking!

Aversive Therapy and Covert Sensitisation
Aversive therapy involves attempting to inhibit a particular response by pairing it with an unpleasant event. This technique has been used in the treatment of alcoholism, smoking, overeating, homosexuality, and various sexual perversions. To many therapists, and clients, aversion therapy is rather distasteful, and the history of its applications in areas like homosexuality particularly so, given that many would consider that this is no longer a deviation.

The main use of hypnosis in this form of behaviour therapy is in replacing a real aversive stimulus such as an electric shock, with an imaginary one, based on a technique known as covert sensitisation (Cautela, 1966, 1967 and 1975). An example of the type of imaginary aversive stimulus used would be nausea. For a client with a problem such as a sexual preference for children this would result in feelings of nausea when the beginnings of a sexual response towards children was felt.

The use of a post-hypnotic suggestion does remove the problem that the client may only experience an aversive stimulus within the clinic, and not outside it, since one problem with aversive therapy, whether hypnosis is used or not, is that many clients develop location-specific responses, i.e. the behaviour is inhibited in the clinic, but not outside it. This is a type of treatment which also raises ethical problems, and some therapists are opposed to it on those grounds. It has always been my opinion that the choice of aversive therapy as the 'right ' therapy for a particular client reveals more about the therapist than the client.

Perhaps the strangest aspect of the use of hypnosis as an adjunct to behaviour therapy is in the incompatibility of the historical development of each. Behaviourism, with its emphasis on objective measures of behaviour, is being used with a phenomenon which often has no apparent overt behaviour associated with it, apart from a relaxed appearance. Nevertheless, in clinical situations there are some interesting applications, e.g. Degun and Degun (1983).

BRIEF HYPNOTHERAPY

Kroger (1977) provides an excellent summary of this type of therapy, which has grown from original work by Erickson (1954). Brief hypnotherapy generally consists of one or a combination of symptom substitution, symptom transformation, symptom amelioration and symptom utilization.

Symptom Substitution

In symptom substitution the aim is to substitute one symptom for another, which should of course be less debilitating than the one which the client originally possessed. Often the crutch provided by the symptom is so important that the client is resistant to any form of therapy which is likely to remove that crutch. However, if the client can be persuaded that the original symptom can be replaced by another which can have the same purpose then less resistance is likely to be encountered. It is the job of the therapist to choose a new symptom and make this acceptable to the client.

There is clearly a lot of skill in choosing the right symptom to act as a substitute. If the symptom is too similar to the original one, then the debilitation will still remain. However, if it is too dissimilar, particularly if it is rather weak and insignificant, then the client may perceive that this symptom cannot possibly do the job of the original one, and be resistant to the substitution. It may be that the best strategy to pursue is to use symptom substitution as a means of removing the most handicapping effects, and to attempt to find out how the symptom is acting as a crutch for the client. It may then be possible to remove the need for the symptom.

Most therapists realize that many symptoms their clients possess are being maintained by a number of factors. For instance a young man who believes he may not be able to satisfy sexually a woman may develop a stammer. He is then able to use this to avoid talking to women, and so he never confronts his real fear. It is generally of crucial importance in bringing about a long term cure for the therapist to understand the factors that are maintaining the problem, and attempt to deal with them.

Symptom Transformation

Symptom transformation is essentially similar to symptom substitution. The difference is that the nature of the symptom is not changed, but the unpleasant quality of the symptom is reduced. An example should make this clear. In the case of an adolescent who continually mutilates himself with his finger nails, a possible symptom transformation would be to replace this form of mutilation with a less severe one, such as nail-biting. Once this transformation has occurred, it is possible to plan and work towards long-term goals, which would generally be to find out the reasons for the problem.

Symptom Amelioration

Symptom amelioration may be used in cases where clients believe they have no control over their symptoms. For example, a man with a severe weight problem which he is convinced he cannot control is instructed not to lose weight, but to gain it. By doing this he sees that his weight is under his control, and is then more able to lose weight.

Symptom Utilization

Symptom utilization consists of making use of the symptom in some way during the therapeutic process. The therapist must accept the client's symptom, particularly when the client believes that the therapist will not do so. This acceptance usually confuses the client, and it may well be possible subsequently to alter some aspect of the behaviour, perhaps the client's perception of the conditions under which the symptom manifests itself.

Brief hypnotherapy is potentially very powerful, but it does require a lot of creative skill on the part of the therapist. It demands close observation and monitoring of the symptom, and also a creative interpretation of the meaning of the symptom for the client.

COUNSELLING

Although it can be argued that counselling itself consists of a whole constellation of therapeutic techniques, within the work of counselling hypnosis can be used along with other techniques. Ross (1981a, 1981b) has outlined some possible uses, particularly in the area of vocational choice. These chiefly involve the use of hypnotic imagery. Cowell and Franklin (1983) have discussed the role of hypnosis in counselling secondary-school pupils, which mostly involves relaxation.

The boundary between counselling and therapy is a very hard one to draw, and may even be something of a pointless exercise. However, the work of the counsellor, whatever that work consists of, may be greatly aided by the use of hypnosis.

FAMILY THERAPY

Ritterman (1983) has written a fascinating book on the uses of hypnosis in family therapy. For anyone who is interested in the applications of hypnosis in this area, this book is invaluable. It is impossible here to do justice to the complexity of family therapy, or to the richness of the techniques used.

Ritterman believes that each individual inhabits and is subject to three contexts. The first of these is the individual's mind-set. This determines rules for accumulating and excluding information and experience, and for arranging, prioritizing and sequencing behaviour, including thoughts, feelings, sensations, and even aspects of physiological life.

The second is the individual's family context. For an individual with a problem, Ritterman argues that one must look for the unit within the family which is responsible for maintaining this situation. The last context is that of the individual's social situation, which includes cultural, racial, religious, gender, class, and generational hierarchies, all of which operate on the individual.

These three contexts all influence the individuals in their perceptions of the other contexts, so although in a particular case the social situation may have the most influence, the way in which this is perceived is partly determined by the individual's mind-set. The symptoms individuals have may be seen as an attempt to reconcile incompatible messages from these three contexts.

Therapy involves attempting to weaken the hold rules from one context exert over another context for the client. This is done by enhancing self-discipline or self-instruction. At the same time the therapist tries to help the client's family reorganize in ways which lessen the number of conditions which bring about the problem behaviour.

Ritterman believes that symptoms can be produced in the family by other family members in a way which is very similar to the way in which hypnosis is induced. A particular phrase, a certain tone of voice, even a particular look, may be sufficient to produce an occurrence of the symptom. It is not surprising then, to find hypnosis advocated as a useful technique in family therapy. According to Ritterman there are five goals which hypnosis can accomplish if needed.

The first is to demonstrate to other observing family members other aspects of the client of which they were unaware. This may allow them to perceive the client in a different way. The second use of hypnosis is to change the client's behaviour at a time when the problem behaviour is about to occur as a result of being triggered by something within the family. Instead of the violent outburst being triggered by a particular comment, the comment now comes to trigger some other form of behaviour, such as an inward musing on some particular subject.

The third use is to make family members immune to each other's harmful suggestions. A fourth possibility is to suggest (within hypnosis) that a particular family event is occurring. All members of the family thus imagine this happening. Indirect suggestions are also given about how this event can be brought about. Afterwards, the family are asked to try to work towards this event, and make it happen. The fifth use described by Ritterman is in the establishment of new domains of privacy for the individual, which cannot be intruded into by other members of the family.

Although here I have been drawing heavily on the work of Ritterman, this does not mean that family therapists should restrict their use of hypnosis to those areas outlined above. On the contrary, within the richness of family therapy, there are many more areas where hypnosis can be most helpful. It is part of the work of the family therapist to find those areas and apply hypnosis creatively to them. On the other hand, for those family therapists new to the use of hypnosis, Ritterman's book itself will provide a new and creative approach to therapy.

HYPNODRAMA

Kroger (1977) notes that it is possible to use psychodrama while the client is under hypnosis. A drama can be scripted, and under hypnosis it is suggested that the client play a particular role. The normal procedures of psychodrama can then be followed.

There are at least two potential advantages of using hypnosis in this way. One is that the client is more likely to follow the suggestions the therapist makes about the way the drama should proceed. The other is that the therapist can suggest that the client has amnesia for some aspects of the psychodrama after it has ended. This can serve to protect the client from things which cannot yet be faced, and it also allows the therapist to reveal certain aspects of the drama a little at a time. The order in which events unfold in the drama may not be the best order from the point of view of the therapeutic process. At the moment there seems to be little work in this area which overtly makes use of hypnosis, but it seems likely that this will change.

I am aware that there are a whole variety of other therapeutic approaches in which hypnosis can play a part which are not covered here. However, I hope I have provided at least a brief introduction to the range of applications of hypnosis. The limitations of hypnosis within a therapeutic situation are essentially the limits imposed by the therapist's imagination.

As I have observed above, the boundaries between different types of therapies are not mutually exclusive. This is true not only for the rather artificial purpose of writing about them, but also for their real use. To a greater or lesser extent all therapists are eclectic in their approach. This need for eclecticism is forced on even the most reluctant therapist by the diversity of clients. The therapist who slavishly follows a particular form of therapy irrespective of the individual client and the corresponding situation is unlikely to be carrying out therapy as effectively as a therapist who varies the therapy to meet the particular demands of the situation, nor enjoying the work as much.

In reality of course no therapist can be other than eclectic, although of course the degree of eclecticism varies tremendously. Therapists are simply people taking part in a relationship with other people, who get called clients, or patients. Whatever theoretical orientation is adopted by the therapist, the demands of the relationship need to be fulfilled, and in fulfilling these demands the therapist must be eclectic. Sometimes, because of their problems, clients cannot be eclectic in their approach to relationships. If the therapist, the other party in the relationship, denies the need for eclecticism, neither person will ever really take part in the relationship, and as Oatley (1984) says, taking part is all there is.

CLINICAL APPLICATIONS OF HYPNOSIS

For many the crucial question regarding hypnosis is: 'what are its clinical applications?' For the rest of this chapter I will attempt to give some answers to this question.

112

Categorizing the areas of application is extremely difficult, and rather than follow any particular classification which is almost certain to be unsatisfactory, I have opted for a simple alphabetical organization.

No doubt some readers will find their favourite areas of application dealt with in a cursory fashion, or even omitted altogether. For this I apologize. However I hope that all readers will learn a little more about the potential applications of hypnosis in a variety of areas outside their own specialization.

Alcoholism
A number of writers, e.g. Kroger (1977) have outlined a number of ways in which hypnosis can be used in the treatment of alcoholism. Suggestions that alcohol tastes awful are perhaps the most common, often coupled with strong suggestions to attend meetings of Alcoholics Anonymous. Interestingly, these meetings sometimes seem like group hypnosis sessions.

Wadden and Anderton (1982) have reviewed a number of studies in which hypnosis has been used with alcoholic patients. They are unable to conclude that hypnosis is of any additional help in the treatment of alcoholism, arguing that such therapeutic success as occurs is probably due to non-hypnotic factors. However, they also emphasize that there are relatively few well-designed studies in this area, so it is far from certain that hypnosis is never going to be of use in this area. Wadden and Penrod (1981) believe that hypnosis might be more helpful if it were used in the stages of the recovery process from alcoholism. For the therapist interested in this application, Kroger (1977) provides a good introduction, and some interesting ideas.

Allergies
There are a variety of types of allergic reaction, e.g. asthma, skin problems etc. Certain of these are susceptible to hypnosis, and these will be discussed later.

Anaesthesia
One of the early uses of hypnosis was in anaesthesia (Esdaile, 1850). Although hypnosis has none of the

113

side effects associated with chemical agents of anaesthesia, unfortunately it does not have the same effectiveness (approaching one hundred per cent for chemical anaesthetics). According to Udolf (1981) only about twenty-five per cent of the population are capable of developing a degree of hypnotically induced anaesthesia sufficient for relatively minor operations, such as tooth extractions and fracture settings. Only about ten per cent of the population can experience hypnotic anaesthesia sufficiently well to undergo major surgery.

Given the almost total effectiveness of chemical anaesthetics, it may appear at first that there is no need for hypnotically induced anaesthesia. However, occasionally chemical agents may not be available, or perhaps the patient is allergic to them. There are also other potential advantages. It may be desirable for the patient to be conscious and in communication with the surgeon, and it also allows for suggestions to be made to facilitate recovery.

Although it is probably required only occasionally, there is no doubt that hypnosis can be an invaluable method of inducing anaesthesia in those patients who are susceptible enough. For those who are sceptical about the possibility of anyone undergoing major surgery under hypnotically induced anaesthesia, it is worth recalling that many internal organs have relatively few pain receptors. The major pain is inflicted by the surgeon's initial incision, and even this is perhaps not so painful as one might expect. It is perhaps the thought of the pain which is so distressing, and the idea of being conscious throughout a major operation.

Nor is it necessarily the case that much preparation is required. With the person who is capable of experiencing anaesthesia under hypnosis only one or two introductory sessions may be needed. Subsequent inductions can be done rapidly, often making use of a post-hypnotic suggestion. Perhaps the surgeon feels more discomfort operating on a conscious patient than the patient who is being operated on. It may be this which has resulted in such relatively little use in this area.

Anorexia Nervosa
This is a very serious problem which is characterized by severe loss of appetite and corresponding weight loss. Death may result. Kroger (1977) reports that hypnosis has been used

successfully in this area. However, further studies are required before any firm conclusions can be drawn.

Anxiety

Most people feel anxious at some time in their lives. For some the anxiety is so severe that they feel the need to seek professional help. Some feel anxious about their work, their future, their family, their friends, or their lack of friends. Some feel anxious but have no idea what they are anxious about. For most of the time this anxiety can be controlled by a number of coping strategies, but occasionally it can no longer be controlled. Then it controls us. It may develop into a panic attack, with accompanying physiological symptoms. Whatever the course, the individual who is prepared to seek help is worthy of receiving it.

Not only is anxiety itself an unpleasant experience, it usually hinders people doing what they want to do. The person who experiences a normal amount of anxiety about exams will not suffer as a result of that anxiety, but the person who cannot revise for worrying about them will. The man who is anxious about whether he will be able to maintain an erection will almost certainly be unable to. Being anxious about the future stops us enjoying the present.

One particularly severe form of anxiety is a phobia. Phobias come in many forms, even the fear of fear itself. Hypnosis can often be used in the treatment of phobias, along with other techniques, such as covert desensitisation (Daniels, 1976), and systematic desensitisation (Kraft, 1984). Hart (1984) reports two cases where hypnotic age regression was used with some success. The techniques used by clinicians tend to reflect their own theoretical viewpoints, although most therapists are now prepared to be more eclectic in their approach.

Anxiety can also lead to more serious physiological problems, such as asthmatic attacks, dermatitis, gastric ulcers, etc. It is crucial that anxiety levels are reduced in these cases. Wilkinson (1984) has outlined an interesting approach to the treatment of anxiety, concentrating on the control of hyperventilation, which appears to have been quite successful. The treatment of anxiety using hypnosis often involves ego-strengthening, and relaxation. Fewtrell (1984) has discussed a number of psychological approaches to anxiety management.

In the case of students with excessive anxiety about exams, I have concentrated on teaching a relaxation technique, usually the clenched fist technique (Stein, 1963). In this technique the fist becomes more and more tightly clenched as the rest of the body relaxes. After a few demonstrations of this using hypnosis, clients practice on their own. The aim is to reduce the time for relaxation to an interval small enough for the clients to relax in real life situations without anyone else being aware of what they are doing. I find that with adequate practice most clients can relax in a very few seconds using this technique.

Along with this physical relaxation I attempt to produce feelings of mental calm by suggesting the person imagines a scene which they enjoy and feel calm and confident in. This is done in such a way that it is associated with the end of the physical relaxation procedure. When the person physically relaxes, these images rapidly occur and produce corresponding feelings of calm and confidence. As far as is possible I try not to make this technique specific to any particular situation, but rather encourage the person to employ it whenever they feel anxious. I have found that this technique works well for students with exam-related anxiety.

Arthritis and Rheumatism
Many sufferers from rheumatism get little or no relief from chemical analgesics. If this is so, then it may be worth trying hypnosis. In addition many patients with arthritis suffer from rather unpleasant side effects from the drugs they are taking. If by using hypnosis they can obtain relief with no drugs at all, or at least cut down their intake, then it would seem sensible to try it. Simply teaching a relaxation technique may well give considerable relief.

Asthma
As Wadden and Anderton (1982) remark, the causes of asthma are not clear (Snider, 1978). However, it is more than likely that there is a complex interaction of psychological, infective and allergic factors. Which of these is considered the most important depends on which authority one reads. Maher-Loughnan (1970) reports that in three controlled studies involving over four hundred asthmatic patients,

significantly more patients in the hypnosis groups showed improvement than was the case for the control groups. Although it is not possible to establish what particular aspect(s) of hypnosis was responsible for the difference, ego-strengthening, self hypnosis and confidence in recovery seem to be the factors worth investigating.

Gardner and Olness (1981) review a number of studies involving the use of hypnosis with children suffering from asthma. They appear unconvinced about the general effectiveness of hypnosis in this area. As is the case in many clinical studies involving hypnosis, it seems unclear how many in the various 'hypnosis' groups were actually hypnotized, and whether perhaps some in the control groups were actually hypnotized.

It is also here, as in so many areas, that the problem of the relationship between hypnotic depth and the therapeutic result occurs. The basis of this problem is quite straightforward. In some areas it seems that the depth of hypnosis is directly related to its effectiveness, e.g. hypnotically induced anaesthesia (Bowers, 1976). Gill and Brenman (1959) have argued that there is no correlation between the depth of trance and the therapeutic benefit. This is an area well worthy of further investigation. In the use of hypnosis in treating asthma this problem is apparent too.

Maher-Loughnan (1970) claimed that there was no correlation between trance depth and clinical responses. Collison (1975), in a retrospective analysis of asthmatic patients, found that only six per cent of light hypnosis subjects were improved, compared with over sixty per cent of deep hypnosis subjects. These two findings seem totally at odds with one another. However, on closer examination there are so many variables involved that it is not too difficult to find possible explanations for these differences.

One problem is that the type and severity of condition may have been different. Another is that the induction process may (in fact almost certainly will) have been different. Perhaps the major difficulty is in deciding what 'improvement' is. This is always a very difficult clinical judgement, and a very objective set of criteria is required if different clinicians are to come to the same conclusion. Whenever these criteria are lacking, it is only to be expected that differences such as these will occur.

The issue of the relationship between hypnotic

depth and therapeutic benefit is one which occurs for all areas of therapy, and, as shown above, throws up some interesting contradictions. Most writers appear to have considered that the relationship between hypnotic depth and outcome is linear, i.e. the deeper the hypnosis, the more effective is the therapy. However, this is not the only possibility. It may be that hypnotic depth is best viewed as having a number of thresholds rather than as a linear scale. For instance, it may be that for a particular therapeutic procedure involving hypnosis, a certain depth of trance is required. If this is exceeded the therapy is likely to work, but it is quite irrelevant how much this depth is exceeded by, the therapy is just as effective.

This threshold almost certainly varies from problem to problem. When a researcher investigates this problem, it is obviously difficult to know where this threshold is. It may be that only a light depth of trance is required for a particular therapy for a particular problem, or it may be that a deep trance is required. Whatever the trance depth required, the difficulty lies in knowing where it is. The way to discover this for any problem is to measure trance depth and susceptibility, and measure outcome, using a number of objective criteria. Then a discriminant analysis can be carried out to establish the trance depth which appears to discriminate best between those patients who reach an objectively defined successful outcome, and those who do not. Once a necessary depth level has been suggested for a particular form of therapy, it can be checked by other researchers in the course of their therapy.

Cardiovascular Disorders
Kroger (1977) argues cogently that hypnosis has a role to play in the treatment of cardiovascular disorders. He emphasizes that there is often a stress factor in these disorders, and simply being told that it would help to relax more is often as useful as telling a phobic patient to stop worrying about the phobic object. Hypnosis is seen as an ideal way to bring about relaxation, and of course the patient can be taught a suitable relaxation technique for use outside the clinic.

He also makes the point that in those disorders with a psychosomatic component, such as essential hypertension, patients are often depressed, anxious, and not at ease with themselves and others. Since these behaviour patterns are likely to be a factor in the disorder, it is sensible to attempt to treat them as well, wherever possible. Hypnosis may well be an appropriate way of dealing with these problems, particularly if it is already being used as a means of relaxing the patient.

Cancer

One of the chief uses of hypnosis in this area is as a means of removing, or at least reducing, the unpleasant side effects of the drugs used in chemotherapy. Generally the most unpleasant effect of these cytotoxic drugs is severe nausea and vomiting, which usually starts about one hour after the injection, and may last for up to twenty-four hours. However, often the sights, sounds and smells of the location where the injection takes place become strongly associated with the feelings of nausea, and become sufficient to induce it. Redd and Andrykowski (1982) conclude that this happens in at least one quarter of all patients undergoing chemotherapy.

One of the methods which has been used to alleviate this difficulty is hypnosis. Studies by LaBaw, Holton, Tewell and Eccles (1975) and Walker (1984a) detail how hypnosis can be used to alleviate this problem. Since feeling nauseous in the clinic before the injection is clearly a conditioned response, it is surprising that there are not more attempts to deal with this by using hypnotically based behaviour therapy. Walker used a number of suggestions to increase confidence and relaxation, and to decrease feelings of nausea and embarrassment, and he also reports that a further study in this area is under way in Aberdeen.

Hilgard and Morgan (1978) have obtained some success in using hypnosis for pain relief with cancer sufferers, as has Olness (1981). The use of hypnosis in this area for suitable patients can be especially beneficial, given the type and quantity of drugs such patients often need. Olness and Gardner (1981) discuss the use of certain imagery techniques to alter the course of the disease process. While it is not currently possible to state that this has any positive effect on the course of the disease, it certainly has no negative effects, and the patients often feel more relaxed, hopeful and able to cope.

Childbirth

Most expectant mothers in the British Isles have the opportunity to attend antenatal classes. Typically these classes include training in a relaxation procedure to help during labour. A number of mothers have reported to me that the relaxation procedure they carried out seemed very similar to a hypnotic induction procedure. In addition, their resulting subjective experiences were very similar. The relationship between hypnosis and relaxation has been discussed previously, but it is interesting that one technique in a particular application has almost universal acceptance, while a very similar one is used relatively little.

In a recent review Fee and Reilley (1982) conclude that the benefits of hypnosis in this area outweigh the disadvantages. Hilgard and Hilgard (1983) believe that for many women hypnosis is a suitable way of preparing for labour. Moon and Moon (1984) used hypnosis to help reduce the mother's pain during childbirth. This is a particularly interesting report because it is written from the point of view of the mother (Hilary Moon) with additional comments from the hypnotist (Tim Moon).

One of the most obvious uses of hypnosis in childbirth is for aiding relaxation. Interestingly, Furneaux and Chapple (1964) found that a group of women prepared by hypnosis judged labour as less unpleasant than a group prepared by relaxation. In addition labour did not last so long, notably the first phase. By using suggestion and imagery it is possible to simulate some of the effects of childbirth for those who are anxious about it, and thereby reduce their anxiety.

In using hypnosis as an analgesic care must be taken to ensure that not all sensation is removed. The sensations of pain are often important for the mother and helpers to understand what stage the labour is in, and whether everything is proceeding smoothly. Rather than removing all sensations, it is preferable either to reduce them to manageable intensities, or to reinterpret them as a different type of sensation other than pain.

Hilgard and Hilgard (1983) outline a number of ways of using hypnosis to relieve the pain of childbirth. One of the most interesting is to suggest that as the painful abdominal contractions occur the mother clenches her fist, and concentrates increasingly on displacing the feelings from her abdomen to her fist. The aim is for the woman to concentrate entirely on the clenching of her fist, shifting her attention completely away from her abdominal contractions.

One final point about hypnosis is that it is probably the safest analgesic. Virtually all chemical analgesics have a small element of risk associated with them, for the unborn child as well as the mother. There are no side effects for the mother with hypnosis, and the child is totally unaffected.

Dentistry

Moss (1977) lists a number of potential uses of hypnosis in dentistry. These are: patient relaxation, alleviation of dental-related fears and anxieties, pain reduction, prevention of gagging, control of bleeding and salivary flow, and reduction of post-operative pain and shock. Udolf (1981) points out that many dental patients have a relatively long lasting professional relationship with their dentist, unlike any other medical practitioner, except perhaps their general practitioner. If a patient is introduced to the benefits of hypnosis early in this relationship, much benefit can potentially be gained.

There are a number of potential problems in the use of hypnosis by dentists. One is that the patient may have some psychological problem which being hypnotized gives them the freedom to reveal. Since they are not qualified to deal with this, and it is really not possible effectively to screen patients for this, dentists must be aware that this is a possibility, albeit remote, and know what course of action to take. Such action would generally be advising the patient to seek help from another professional.

Another difficulty is that dentists may be tempted to treat dental phobia. It is a mistake to think that a dental phobia is actually a dental problem; it is a psychological problem in which the phobic object is the dentist, the drill, etc. Although the chances of harming the patient are remote, professional ethics should demand that the treatment of psychological problems is left to the right professional agency.

A similar problem exists with bruxism. Most individuals who grind their teeth excessively are extremely tense and carry a lot of suppressed rage, according to Moss (1977). Although some therapists may see this as a little extreme, it is probably true that bruxism is better treated by a therapist with psychological training.

Two areas which are particularly interesting are pain relief and gagging. As reported by Gerschman, Burrows and Fitzgerald (1981) gagging can affect individuals in a number of ways. It may make the wearing of dentures impossible, make dental work extremely difficult, and even make tooth brushing impossible. Gerschman et al list a variety of types of treatment which have been used for this difficulty. These include local anaesthetics, breathing exercises, and tranquillizers. From this it can be concluded that there is no effective recognized method for dealing with this problem.

Perhaps because of this there has been considerable interest in the use of hypnosis to control the gagging reflex. Moss (1977) has made much use of waking suggestions, and is confident of a seventy-five per cent success rate. Erickson, Herschman and Secter (1961) and Ament (1971) both mention cases which indicate that one of the reasons for gagging lies in traumatic experiences in the past. Methods used to deal with this include suggestion, time distortion, and a range of behaviouristic techniques. There seems little doubt that the use of hypnosis in this specialized area of dentistry is likely to increase.

Hilgard and Hilgard (1983) review the use of hypnosis to relieve pain in dentistry. They believe that pain in dental procedures is very difficult to separate from other problems such as anxiety, e.g. the more anxious the patients are the more pain they are likely to feel. The level of pain can therefore be reduced indirectly by tackling other problems such as anxiety, or directly by dealing with the pain itself.

Hilgard and Hilgard (1983) review a number of studies in which hypnosis was used as the sole anaesthetic. Their conclusion is that hypnosis may be a useful substitute for chemical anaesthetics, and that the more 'hypnotizable' the patient the less pain will be felt. Their final comment on the use of hypnosis to relieve dental pain is that, for the majority of patients, chemical anaesthetics are quite satisfactory. However, if these are unsuitable on medical grounds, or if the patient is morally opposed to them, hypnosis is likely to be a good substitute.

In conclusion, it is unfortunate that hypnosis is not used more in dentistry. It is well suited to deal with a number of problems which arise in dentistry, from dental phobia to gagging.

Furthermore, the long-term professional relationship which usually develops between the dentist and the patient would be expected to facilitate the use of hypnosis. As Kent (1906) observes, more controlled studies of the use of hypnosis in dentistry are needed.

Dermatology

There are a variety of skin disorders, such as eczema, psoriasis, acne, pruritus, herpes and warts. Many of these have a psychological component, and are often triggered or made worse by psychological states such as anxiety. Hypnosis has been used in the treatment of all these types of dermatological problems, with some success.

One technique which Kroger (1977) reports as being useful with excessive itching is symptom amelioration, followed by symptom substitution. It is suggested that the patient try to make the itching worse, thus demonstrating some control over it. Next the symptom can be transferred to another part of the body, and reduced in intensity. Olness (1970) describes a case in which intense itching was reduced by using imagery, specifically by images of snow, which, as well as diverting attention away from the itching, may have induced feelings of coolness as well.

Imagery has also been used in the treatment of psoriasis (Kline, 1953). Since psoriasis is often alleviated by exposure to the sun, suggestions are made that the patient is sunbathing, with attendant feelings of warmth. This is usually done with different parts of the body in turn, until as much of the body as necessary can be treated in this way.

Wadden and Anderton (1982) review a number of studies of the use of hypnosis to remove warts. Warts are thought to be caused by viruses, and they are known to be very sensitive to skin conditions. The most common hypnotic technique is to suggest tingling feelings in the area surrounding the wart. It is thought that this increases the blood flow, and that this environment is less suitable for the wart virus, and the wart gradually disappears. However, it is not clear whether the virus has permanently disappeared, or is still present awaiting the correct conditions for renewed growth.

Despite these unknowns hypnosis does seem to be a very useful technique. Although it is not clear whether an induction procedure is really necessary, there appears to be a positive relationship between wart remission and hypnotizability. A number of studies, e.g. Sinclair-Gieben and Chalmers (1959) and Hellier (1951) have shown the importance of suggestion in this area. Folk remedies, such as 'selling' warts to another person also make use of suggestion. It is clear that any technique, such as hypnosis, which makes use of suggestion, is likely to be valuable in the treatment of warts. This seems to be particularly true if the patient is susceptible, which is much as one might expect.

Skin disorders are particularly interesting to treat by hypnosis, for they often have a mixed aetiology. Although most have a large organic component, it is often the case that particular psychological conditions, e.g. fear, may be crucial in triggering or exacerbating a particular condition. In addition the physiological conditions necessary for the disorder to occur may be quite restricted, and by altering the psychological state, or by bringing about by suggestion small changes in the local physiological conditions, the problem may be greatly reduced, or disappear altogether. These problems also allow for some very creative uses of hypnosis, which is very beneficial for the jaded therapist!

Diabetes
As is true for many illnesses, diabetes may be made much worse by stressful life events. In fact in some persons stress may trigger the initial occurrence of the disorder. Hypnosis is clearly one possible way of reducing the stress, and hence the diabetes. Patients suffering from diabetes may also have circulatory problems, which can lead to feelings of cold and pain in their extremities. Grabowska (1971) used hypnosis to bring about relaxation and changes in blood flow, which relieved symptoms caused by poor circulation in over fifty per cent of diabetic patients.

There are also a number of factors associated with diabetes and its treatment which may cause psychological distress for the patient. These include the invasive nature of the treatment when insulin injections are required, and often resentment directed at one or both parents for having what some patients regard as a genetic weakness from which they are suffering. Counselling is often of help here, but in some cases, e.g. needle phobia, hypnosis may be a valuable way of dealing with this problem.

Gastrointestinal Disorders

Many gastrointestinal disorders are at least partially due to emotions such as anxiety, and no doubt many readers will be able to recall their own visceral reactions to stressful situations. Hypnosis has been used to treat a number of these disorders, such as irritable bowel syndrome, peptic ulcers, constipation and post-gastrectomy syndrome. Kroger (1977) reports a number of studies which have apparently successfully treated the latter condition most effectively.

Walker (1984b) outlines the use of relaxation and post-hypnotic suggestion in the treatment of irritable bowel syndrome. In these two cases a variety of post-hypnotic suggestions were used, including more control of symptoms and ego strengthening. Considerable success was achieved with both these patients, who actually presented with quite different symptoms, one having poor control over defaecation, and the other severe intestinal pain. The objective measures used in this study are such that considerable confidence can be attached to the results.

Many children suffer from abdominal pains which appear to have no organic cause; in fact very often it is impossible to discern any cause at all. These abdominal pains may recur frequently, causing genuine distress to the child concerned. Gardner and Olness (1981) describe the uses of hypnosis in treating this problem. They report that hypnosis is often used as a last resort rather than as the treatment of choice, so it is even more to the credit of the clinician using hypnosis that there has been some success with this approach.

This is of course a problem which bedevils many clinicians who use hypnosis. It is quite common to get letters of referral which request some therapeutic use of hypnosis for a patient for whom nothing else has worked. The success rate for hypnosis would probably be rather higher for a variety of disorders if hypnotherapeutic techniques were used with patients who had not been unsuccessfully treated a number of times already.

Gynaecology

Miller (1979) describes the uses of hypnosis with a number of different gynaecological conditions. These include menstrual and premenstrual cramps, amenorrhea (lack of menstruation), pseudocyesis (false pregnancy), functional dysmenorrhea

(difficult or painful menstruation), functional
uterine bleeding, pruritis vulvae and vaginae
(excessive itching), functional leucorrhea (vaginal
discharge), functional sterility and menopause.
Miller's approach seems to be to look for the
unconscious causes of these problems, and most of
the case studies he describes illustrate what might
be described as a hypnoanalytic technique.
What is often called premenstrual tension may
be alleviated by hypnotherapeutic techniques. This
affects many women, and although most have developed
a number of coping strategies, learning a relaxation
technique, with or without hypnosis, can reduce the
amount of tension considerably.

Hyperhidrosis
Excessive sweating is an unpleasant problem which is
often related to anxiety, and may therefore be
reduced if the anxiety is reduced. Hypnosis is
obviously one method by which the anxiety can be
alleviated. Ambrose (1952) also relates a case where
hyperhidrosis in a boy of thirteen appeared to be
related to a traumatic incident which happened five
years previously. This was discovered using
hypnotically induced age regression, and after
several more sessions the problem disappeared.

Inadequacy
Inadequacy is best thought of as a feeling of being
unable to cope with everyday situations. Generally
associated with this is a lack of self-confidence.
Stanton (1981) used an induction procedure coupled
with ego enhancement to deal with this problem. In
what appears to have been a well designed study,
Stanton concludes that this treatment was more
effective than that received by the control group,
which consisted of discussing ways of gaining more
control over their lives, although the patients in
this group showed some improvement too.

Insomnia
Being unable to sleep can be a very depressing (and
tiring) experience. Most individuals experience this
at different times during their lives, but for some
individuals insomnia is a chronic problem. Insomnia
may also take different forms. Some find falling
asleep extremely difficult, whereas others wake up
and cannot get back to sleep. A pattern of early

morning wakening is often associated with depression.

Simple post-hypnotic suggestion that self-hypnosis will merge into sleep may be sufficient in some cases to restore the normal pattern of sleep. However, in other cases more complex uses of hypnosis are required, and where insomnia is associated with depression, other forms of treatment altogether may be required.

Migraine
Migraine is a disorder involving severe head pain, often accompanied by nausea and intense dislike of noise and bright light. Migraine varies greatly in its characteristics, severity and frequency, and perhaps because of this there seems to be no widely accepted definition for it. There have been attempts to classify different types of migraine, but no overall agreement. One attempt by Budzynski (1979) describes seven types of migraine, some of which are more common than others.

A survey by Waters and O'Connor (1971) revealed that about a quarter of the population can expect to suffer from migraine. Perhaps the most frequent type is common migraine, which seems to be characterized by bilateral pain and gradual onset and lack of prodromata (warning signs) such as blurred vision and difficulty in focusing. Classical migraine usually has prodromata associated with it, and is generally unilateral, whereas cluster migraine consists of unilateral headaches which follow one another in rapid succession.

The aetiology of migraine is not clear. It has been hypothesized that the dilation of cerebral blood vessels is responsible for the onset of migraine attacks (Bakal, 1975). It has also been suggested (Sovak, Kunzel, Sternbach and Dalessio, 1978) that sufferers from migraine may have a generalized vasomotor dysfunction. Alladin (1984) believes that use of hypnosis, along with other more psychological forms of treatment was engendered by the relative failure of drug regimes for migraine patients. However, there are relatively few published studies of the use of hypnosis in the treatment of migraine, and those that do exist are not all tightly designed experimental studies.

Perhaps the best is the study by Alladin (1984). This involved fifty migraine sufferers who were randomly allocated to one of five conditions. Several important findings arose from this study.

The most important was that two conditions, hypnotherapy involving induction of warmth, and active progressive relaxation, appeared to be most effective in the treatment of severe chronic migraine. Another finding was that glove anaesthesia appears to act on the perception of pain rather than on the mechanism of migraine. Alladin's final recommendation is that for chronic migraine the treatment of choice should be psychological.

Narcotic Addiction

Narcotic addiction affects a wide variety of individuals, from teenagers to the elderly. Generally the motivation leading to the addiction differs, with teenagers taking drugs initially to find out what type of experience results, while in older persons the drugs are usually prescribed to deal with a problem such as insomnia or depression. Typically these latter drugs are barbiturates.

The nature of addiction is a very complex process. There may be physiological addiction, psychological addiction, or both. Some drugs may prove addictive to some users, but not to others. However, whatever the nature of the addiction, by the time addicts arrive in the clinic they are in need of assistance.

Kroger (1977) states that hypnosis has not been effective in the treatment of narcotic addiction. However, he does believe that it is useful in the alleviation of withdrawal symptoms. In contrast Baumann (1970) found that with patients who are well motivated to change, hypnosis appeared to be a useful treatment adjunct. This seemed to be particularly true if they perceived the drugs to be physically dangerous. Diment (1981) reports that relaxation produced via hypnosis was effective in reducing the number of barbiturates taken in a 59-year-old woman with anxiety and obsessional thoughts.

Despite the relative paucity of successful uses of hypnosis in this area, this does not mean that it is not going to have some success in the future. As in many cases where hypnosis is a useful adjunct to treatment, finding the appropriate techniques is dependent upon the creative ability of the therapist, who suddenly becomes aware of a new possibility.

Neuromuscular Disorders
Kroger (1977) devotes a chapter to the use of hypnosis in the physical rehabilitation of neuromuscular disorders. These disorders include multiple sclerosis, poliomyelitis, Parkinson's disease, and cerebral palsy. It is Kroger's belief that the relearning necessary for rehabilitation to occur can be facilitated by hypnosis. Certainly there are a number of case studies which have produced encouraging results, such as that by Lazar (1977), who employed hypnosis in the treatment of a 12-year-old cerebral palsied child, and Kroger (1977) who used hypnosis in the treatment of a 34-year old woman who had had polio as a child. It is possible that hypnosis may well be used increasingly in the rehabilitation process in this area. However, at the moment, well designed, controlled studies are rather lacking. It should also be noted that hypnosis is being used here very much as an adjunct to therapy; the treatment may take place during hypnosis, perhaps to aid attention, or hypnosis may be used to help with associated factors, for instance to aid the patient relax.

Obesity
Helping people stop smoking and lose weight seem to be among the most common uses of hypnosis. This is particularly the case among 'hypnotherapists' who advertise in newspapers and shop windows, and sometimes make quite outrageous claims about their 'cure rates'. It is particularly interesting to note, therefore, that Wadden and Anderton (1982) in their comprehensive review of studies in this area found little evidence that hypnosis was of unique value in weight reduction.

There have been a number of approaches used within hypnosis to help people lose weight. These include psychotherapeutic techniques, in which an attempt is made to uncover the cause of the obesity, aversive conditioning and direct suggestion. Although a number of studies, e.g. Stanton (1976), reported successful findings, it is not clear that success was due to the hypnotic induction procedure. On the contrary, it seems that factors such as expectancy, motivation, encouragement and dietary advice are just as important, if not more so, and at least some of these are present in hypnosis.

As experienced clinicians and researchers will realize, this is a typical problem in experimental design, which is more intrusive in clinical studies of treatment effectiveness than elsewhere. Generally it is almost impossible to control all variables apart from the one the experimenter wishes to manipulate. To illustrate the enormity of this task, consider the following example. If the aim is to compare suggestion following an induction procedure with suggestion without an induction procedure, then one must try to have a therapist who believes each approach is equally effective, otherwise the expectancy of the therapist can be communicated to the patients, if not directly, at least by subtle, non-verbal cues. Even if such a person can be found, a whole host of other problems of experimental design remain to be solved. In fact, I do not believe any experimental design can be perfect, although some are certainly better than others.

Opthalmology
There have been a number of applications of hypnosis within this area, including eye surgery, orthoptics, glaucoma and adjustment to contact lenses.
    One particularly interesting use is with children with suppression amblyopia. This is a condition in which the visual images of the two eyes do not fuse to form one image. The image from one eye is suppressed, and the image from the other eye is the only one perceived. Two studies, Browning and Crasilneck (1957) and Browning, Quinn and Crasilneck (1958) have both reported results which are encouraging. It appears that suggestion under hypnosis brought about an improvement in vision in the non-seeing eye.
    It is surprising that so little research has been carried out on the uses of hypnosis in opthalmology, given the number of areas in which there have been encouraging reports. No doubt in the future there will be an increase in the use of hypnosis in this area, particularly with children.

Orthopaedics
Hypnosis has been used in a number of orthopaedic problems. Olness and Gardner (1981) present two interesting case studies on the use of hypnosis to facilitate recovery after a fracture, and following amputation. Hypnosis can also be used in the treatment of torticollis. Since this usually has a large hysterical component it is particularly susceptible to techniques such as hypnosis, and is

in fact often very resistant to physiotherapy. Lower back pain may often be strongly influenced by the psychological state of the patient, and therefore using hypnosis to help treat the emotional state can be worthwhile.

Otology

Miller (1979) believes that hypnosis is a valuable means of relieving tension and anxiety in patients who have problems in this area. Crasilneck and Hall (1975) claim that over fifty per cent of patients with tinnitus are helped by learning to relax using self-hypnosis. Since emotional factors may well be involved in the frequency, duration and severity of bouts of tinnitus, it is surprising that more use has not been made of hypnosis in treating this problem.

Pain

The use of hypnosis in the relief of pain has already been mentioned earlier in various contexts. There is a very large literature on this, and I hope that this brief introduction will at least give readers some insight into the nature of pain and hypnotic approaches to its control.

Pain is a very complex phenomenon, and its investigation is surrounded by difficulties. It is a subjective experience, and generally a person who says he or she is feeling pain has to be believed. There are various physiological measures such as heart rate and galvanic skin response (GSR) which are related to pain, but they certainly do not provide wholly reliable, objective measures of pain.

There are also several different types of pain. One particularly important distinction is between non-clinical and clinical pain. Much work has been done on both these types of pain, and it would be particularly helpful if researchers could be sure that results with one type of pain were valid with the other. However, non-clinical pain is rather different in several respects. It is usually of relatively short duration, and the subject does not experience the depression felt by those with clinical pain.

A variety of methods have been used for inducing non-clinical pain, some of which are extremely unpleasant. They include pressure on bones, produced by wedges and headbands, pain produced by radiant heat, toothache produced by electric current and electric shocks. Hilgard and Hilgard (1983) in their studies have used pain which they have argued is more similar to clinical pain. These are cold pressor pain, which is produced by inserting an arm in ice water, and ischemic pain, which results from exercising a muscle which has little blood in it.

It has proved very difficult to come up with a definition of pain, (Sternbach, 1968). There are many different types of pain, such as 'throbbing', 'dull', 'sharp', 'stabbing', etc. In addition pain may be intractable, or resistant to treatment. Although much pain is related to tissue damage, many pains are not so straightforward in their origin. Some forms of pain do not result from tissue damage, such as migraine. Pain may be psychosomatic in origin, but none the less real for that. Pain may also be referred, i.e. felt in a location other than where the cause of the pain really is. Pain may even be felt in a part of the body which has been amputated; this is known as phantom limb pain, and may be extremely intractable.

Because pain is such a subjective experience, there are many individual differences. Overall pain thresholds vary from one person to another, and indeed pain thresholds vary within the same individual depending on the circumstances. Pain also varies with age, although there is no clear cut relationship.

The theory which best seems to account for the various aspects of pain is the gate control theory, put forward by Melzack and Wall in 1965. This is a very complex theory, which is in accord with much experimental and clinical work. However, it does have a number of difficulties, which are discussed by Casey (1970 and 1973). The gate theory of pain is constantly being revised, and no doubt will continue to be so.

Hilgard and Hilgard (1983) have shown how useful hypnosis can be in the control of pain. Their laboratory studies have made clear the link between hypnotic susceptibility and pain, and this relationship is also confirmed by other researchers, such as Spanos, Radtke-Bodorik, Ferguson and Jones (1979). There are, however, many methodological difficulties associated with this work, such as the extent to which an hypnotic induction alone reduces pain, without any specific instructions on pain reduction. This, and other problems, are extremely well discussed by Hilgard and Hilgard (1983).

Wadden and Anderton (1982) conclude that hypnosis is effective in the treatment of clinical pain. They also agree with Hilgard and Hilgard (1983) that, in general, there is a positive relationship between hypnotic susceptibility and ability to benefit from hypnotic methods of pain control. Care does need to be taken, however, in differentiating the effects of hypnosis in reducing anxiety and in pain control. These may be very difficult to separate, since the relaxation produced by the induction procedure itself may increase the patient's tolerance to pain. It might perhaps be argued that for the clinician disentangling these effects is not particularly crucial, if the end result is that the patient feels less pain. But for the researcher this can be a very necessary distinction to make.

As should already be apparent from the discussion so far, hypnosis can be used with a wide variety of clinical problems, although it has been argued (Udolf, 1981) that it is more valuable when employed in the control of chronic, organic pain of known aetiology. It may perhaps be more appropriate to argue that psychogenic pain is better dealt with by using hypnotic techniques other than pain reduction, such as analytic techniques.

There are many different techniques which can be employed in the use of hypnosis in the relief of pain. One method is direct suggestion, which in itself may take different forms. The method may be as simple as suggesting that the part affected is getting numb, and can no longer feel pain. Another less direct method is to suggest that the patient is receiving a local anaesthetic, and can then feel the pain gradually disappearing. 'Glove anaesthesia' is also often employed. In this, numbness is suggested in the patient's hand, and it is further suggested that this numbness can be transferred to the part of the body where the pain is by touching it with the anaesthetized hand. A further possibility is to suggest that the patient has a 'switch' to turn off the pain.

Another method is to direct attention away from the pain. This is often referred to as a distraction technique. Here it is suggested that the patient concentrate on a pleasant experience. This pleasant experience can be suggested and described by the therapist, or it can be left entirely to the patient. Sometimes, particularly with children, it can be a good idea to suggest that they are 'viewing' the experience on a television screen.

In contrast to this technique it is sometimes the case that the patient cannot think about anything other than the pain itself. If this is so, then the therapist can suggest that the patient focuses on the pain, but also forms an image of the pain as, for instance, a red light. If the pain is a throbbing pain, then the light can pulse, and suggestions can be given that the pulsing is decreasing in frequency, and as this happens, so the throbbing reduces in frequency.

One technique which is effective in some circumstances is to transfer the pain from one part of the body to another. An advantage of this is that the area chosen for the relocation can be less sensitive, and so the pain is less severe. Also, because the patient has demonstrated some control over the pain, it is often then easier to use other suggestions to remove the pain altogether. Another possibility is to transform the pain into some other type of feeling, such as a tingling sensation. This has advantages where the pain is giving valuable information, such as the contraction pains in childbirth.

One rather unusual technique is dissociation. Here the aim is to separate the patient from the pain. This can be done by suggesting that the part of the body where the pain is located is being separated from the rest of the body, and since there is no connection there can be no pain.

It is also possible to use age regression and take the patient back to a period before the onset of the pain. Another technique which utilizes time manipulation is time distortion. It is suggested that time is passing much more quickly. This technique is particularly useful in surgical pain, where the pain has a definite duration.

Pain is one area in which hypnosis can be extremely useful. However, just because hypnosis often shows success in this area does not mean that care does not have to be taken in its use. As Gibson (1984) observes, some clinical reports are almost unbelievable. The success of hypnosis in the control of pain is still dependent on the skill of the clinician.

Sexual Problems
There are a number of different types of sexual problems, some of which are organic in origin. The majority, however, have psychological causes. Degun and Degun (1982) examined the various uses of

hypnosis in the treatment of sexual problems. They concluded that there are three general categories. The first of these they refer to as 'hypnoanalysis', which they consider to involve mostly age regression and hypnotic abreaction of traumatic events related to the sexual problem.

The second category is also psychoanalytic in orientation, but the therapists have eschewed traditional psychoanalytic techniques, and instead use simpler, more direct methods such as direct suggestion and visual imagery. The third category consists of the behaviour therapists, who use hypnosis as an adjunct to their behavioural techniques e.g. systematic desensitisation.

These various techniques have been used with a wide range of sexual problems. Barabasz (1977) has used post-hypnotic suggestions in the treatment of premature ejaculation, while Degun and Degun (1982) have used hypnotically assisted systematic desensitisation, in combination with other techniques such as joint counselling, in the treatment of vaginismus.

Araoz (1982) has written a particularly interesting book where he discusses the uses of what he refers to as 'The New Hypnosis' in sex therapy. 'The New Hypnosis' is not a radical view, but rather a broad definition of hypnosis to include the use of the imagination by the client, even if no induction procedure has been employed. Araoz describes a number of hypnotic techniques which can be employed by the sex therapist in the treatment of sexual problems. However, he has done rather more than this, and has succeeded in bringing together a number of different approaches which should help the perceptive sex therapist to gain new insights into sexual problems, and also develop new approaches to treatment.

Smoking

As mentioned earlier, one of the most common applications of hypnosis, particularly by lay hypnotists, is to help people stop smoking. Wadden and Anderton (1982) conclude that a person's motivation to stop smoking is the best indicator of success, and that there appears to be no relationship between a reduction in smoking and hypnotic susceptibility. It seems that in many studies which used hypnosis to help people reduce or cease smoking altogether, the successes could well have been due to non-hypnotic factors.

Another interesting finding is that the vast majority of clients who stop smoking do so early in the treatment programme. Sheehan and Surman (1982) found ninety-eight per cent of clients who stopped smoking for any period did so by the end of the second session. This is in line with the conclusion of Cornwell, Burrows and McMurray (1981) that if smokers fail to quit after the first session it is unlikely that further sessions will have much effect.

Sheehan and Surman (1982) also investigated the consequences of stopping smoking. Nearly half of those who tried to stop smoking gained weight, while in the success group this proportion was three quarters. In addition there were psychological changes, which were generally negative. These included increased irritability in nearly half the subjects, anxiety in twenty-one per cent, and depression in a quarter.

No doubt hypnosis will continue to be used in helping people cease smoking, although it is not clear how much hypnosis contributes to any success that takes place. Further studies will help to clarify the precise place of hypnosis (if any) in this area. It is also worth considering what a successful outcome is. Apart from the obvious case where a person stops smoking altogether, a reduction in smoking is also worth achieving. Although it is difficult to decide what is a significant reduction, a twenty per cent reduction is probably the minimum reduction which should be aimed for. Nor should it be considered failure if a person stops smoking for a period of only six months. Researchers and clinicians should recall that a tobacco-free period like this can be an important achievement for some persons, and in addition it may be repeated a number of times in a person's life, when it achieves even more significance.

Speech and Language Problems
There are a number of reported uses of hypnosis in the remediation of speech and language problems. One such area is stammering. Lockhart and Robertson (1977) claim that they cured a group of clients with mild stammers by the use of hypnotherapy alone, specifically ego-strengthening and anxiety reduction by the clenched fist technique (Stein, 1963). A second group with more severe stammers were treated with a combination of hypnotherapy and speech therapy exercises. The authors argue that

hypnotherapy was a crucial factor in the successful treatment of some members of this group. However, it is not clear to what extent any improvements were due to hypnosis, or whether they resulted from other factors.

Laguaite (1976) has investigated the use of hypnosis with children with deviant voices. Hypnosis was used initially to increase motivation, but later was used to help uncover some reasons for the tension. Laguaite reports that the only two children who showed no improvement were the ones she judged to be least responsive to hypnosis.

There are also a number of case studies in other areas of speech therapy. Horsley (1982) used brief hypnotherapy and self-hypnosis with a woman with psychogenic dysphonia, apparently with some success. Mason (1961) used hypnosis to help motivate aphasic patients. He reports that depth of trance appeared unrelated to the results of therapy, but unfortunately no details are given about how trance depth was measured.

Also of interest is a review of the uses of hypnosis in speech pathology and audiology by Rousey (1961). In his summary Rousey concludes that with few exceptions the cases reviewed fail to take into account relevant variables in either hypnosis or speech and hearing. Such comments are still relevant in much clinical work. Speech and language problems are generally very complex problems, and the precise role of hypnosis in their treatment remains to be defined.

PERSONAL REFLECTIONS

There is no doubt that hypnosis can be a valuable adjunct to a whole range of therapeutic techniques. However, there is still considerable difficulty in deciding which problems are most suited to a remedial approach involving hypnosis. Although the standard of research on clinical effectiveness has steadily improved, there are still many areas where there is a great deal of confusion and ignorance.

The problem of clinical evaluation is one which I have alluded to earlier in this chapter. Although research designs have become increasingly more and more sophisticated, and the statistical analyses likewise, the strict scientific approach involving control and manipulation of variables simply cannot always cope with the complexity of human beings. This does not mean that the scientific approach should be abandoned. On the contrary, clinicians should be extremely sensitive to well designed and analysed studies. However, they should be equally sensitive to the individual they are treating. Although some clients may be similar, they are never the same. The skill of the clinician lies in the creative use of therapeutic techniques, while basing this use firmly within existing knowledge.

Perhaps the greatest bar to therapeutic success is rigidity on the part of the therapist. Nothing is necessarily what it seems, and therapists need constantly to monitor their treatment, and be prepared to revise radically both their diagnosis and treatment. An example should help illustrate a number of these points.

Mr. D. complained of sea-sickness, which appeared to have no organic cause. He had been sailing for many years with no episodes of sea-sickness, and had recently bought his own yacht. The sea-sickness was debilitating enough for him to consider selling this yacht. Initial treatment centred on relaxation using the clenched fist technique.

However, during the treatment the client revealed by his comments that he felt his general level of anxiety had increased over the previous few months, and he was worried about meeting deadlines. He hoped that this technique would help him relax. Up until this point, it had been suggested that Mr. D. use the clenched fist technique only when yachting. It was now the therapist's opinion that this needed to be revised, and that the cause of the seasickness, which it had not been possible to discover before, really needed to be investigated further.

Hypnosis was used to regress the client to an episode on his yacht when he had developed sea-sickness. He was instructed to recall specifically his emotions and worries. Later questioning revealed that the only worry Mr. D. had was concerned with whether he would be able to return by the time he had promised. (For those with no knowledge of yachting, it is important to realize that if the conditions are unfavourable it is quite possible to be hours, or even days, late.) He reported that he felt quite guilty about this possibility.

At this point a possible reason for the seasickness was revealed. Whenever Mr. D. felt sea-sick he had to return to port as quickly as possible. The effect of this was that the guilt he felt about the possibility of being late disappeared. Treatment then proceeded on the basis that the purpose of the sea-sickness for the client was to stop him feeling guilty. He was instructed to use the clenched fist technique to relax whenever he felt tense. He was also given a post-hypnotic suggestion that he would not set fixed deadlines for returning from yachting, or in fact for anything, but would be much more flexible.

Five years later Mr. D. was sailing more frequently, and his sea-sickness had disappeared, except when the sea was unusually rough, and even then it was manageable. He reported that he was no longer so worried about keeping deadlines and being bound by the clock.

This case, which I do not consider atypical, illustrates the various twists and turns that therapy can take. The clinician must be constantly aware that the proposed programme of treatment may need to be drastically revised by a single comment from the client. But that is what makes therapy so interesting.

SELECTED READING

There are many books, and many more papers, on clinical approaches. The ones I have chosen represent, I hope, a balanced approach.

Araoz, D. L. (1982) Hypnosis and Sex Therapy, Brunner/Mazel, New York
Although this book deals primarily with sexual problems, its attempts at theoretical and clinical integration make it well worth reading.

Bandler, R. and Grinder, J. (1979) Frogs Into Princes, Real People Press, Moab, Utah
This is probably the most accessible book about Neurolinguistic Programming. Despite the controversial status of this therapeutic approach, it is nevertheless a book to make the reader think carefully about therapy, and about hypnosis.

Gardner, G. G. and Olness, K. (1981) Hypnosis and Hypnotherapy with Children, Grune and Stratton, New York
This is an extremely thorough book on the uses of hypnosis with children. It is also the best written and most enjoyable I have come across on clinical applications of hypnosis.

Haley, J. (1977) <u>Uncommon</u> <u>Therapy:</u> <u>The</u> <u>Psychiatric</u>
<u>Techniques</u> <u>of</u> <u>Milton</u> <u>H.</u> <u>Erickson</u> <u>M.</u> <u>D.</u>,
Norton, New York
This book is about the most imaginative
and innovative hypnotherapist of all time. For
anyone looking for new ideas, this is a good
starting point.

Kroger, W. S. (1977) <u>Clinical</u> <u>and</u> <u>Experimental</u>
<u>Hypnosis</u> <u>in</u> <u>Medicine,</u> <u>Dentistry,</u> <u>and</u>
<u>Psychology,</u> (2nd. Ed.), J. B. Lippincott
Company, Philadelphia
Kroger generally takes an analytic approach to
problems. However, there is tremendous breadth of
coverage in this book, and a mass of references.

Ritterman, M. (1983) <u>Using</u> <u>Hypnosis</u> <u>in</u> <u>Family</u>
<u>Therapy,</u> Jossey-Bass Publishers, San Francisco
Ritterman gives a very detailed approach to using
hypnosis in family therapy. This is a fascinating
area, and this is the book to read.

Chapter Eight

THERAPEUTIC USES OF HYPNOSIS: NON-CLINICAL

This chapter, as its title suggests, is concerned
with non-clinical uses of hypnosis. I recognize that
there is a very fuzzy boundary between clinical and
non-clinical uses of hypnosis. For instance, is the
treatment of creative blocks clinical or non-
clinical?
    Some readers may also see therapeutic uses as
implying clinical uses. I do not subscribe to that
view. Many techniques can be used in clinical and
non-clinical applications. The use of age regression
in attempts to uncover 'forgotten' information is
one such example. This may be part of
psychoanalysis, or of an experiment to investigate
early childhood memories. I also believe that many
definitions of the term 'therapeutic' are too
restrictive. A number of the problems that people
have do not really warrant the description
'clinical', but require some sort of therapy to
overcome them.
    There are lots of problems like this. One is
grief. Sometimes medical practitioners appear too
ready to see grief as a clinical problem and
prescribe tranquillizers to help the person cope.
Grieving is a natural process, and it seems to help
the person come to terms with the loss of a loved
one. The 'therapy' for grief lies within the rituals
attending the funeral service, the disposal of the
person's property, and the support of relatives and
friends.
    Another problem faced by many people is work
created tension and stress. This may develop into a
clinical problem, but many people develop their own
therapeutic strategies such as playing sport,
becoming involved in a hobby, or using specific
relaxation techniques. These are all therapeutic
strategies, which are none-the-less real because

they are developed and carried out by the persons themselves.

A final example will, I hope, illustrate some of the problems involved in deciding what is a clinical problem and what is not. It should also highlight the breadth of the term 'therapeutic'. One of the most common problems (Mitchell, 1982) is phobic fear. The majority of people seek no professional assistance. However, this does not mean they have no coping strategies. On the contrary, they often develop complex coping strategies. These include manipulating others, avoidance, and various methods of reducing tension. For many people phobias only become a problem when these strategies are no longer effective, and the phobia interferes with their social life or their work.

The decision as to when a phobia becomes a clinical problem is therefore at least partly determined by how well the person's own coping strategies are working, or not working. It is also partly determined by the object of the phobic fear. A fear of cars is much more debilitating than a fear of snakes, at least in the U.K. Sometimes a phobia only becomes a clinical problem when a person's own therapeutic strategies no longer work, and they need to turn elsewhere for therapy.

For the rest of the chapter a number of different areas will be examined where hypnosis is helpful to people. It is perhaps in these areas that it is hardest for people to obtain professional help. No doubt many of the hypnotists who advertise in the local papers and shop windows are seeking help for these types of problems. There is also much less published work in this area, so effectiveness is very difficult to judge.

Gibbons (1979) devotes a whole chapter to improving creativity and performance. He suggests that a whole range of different areas may be improved by hyperempiria (heightened arousal induced by hypnotic techniques) or other hypnotic procedures. One such area is academic performance. Gibbons gives a number of detailed suggestions for improving study skills, taking examinations and facilitating class participation. This is an area which could expand dramatically. I have helped a number of students reduce the anxiety they feel while taking exams, but these students have been experiencing anxiety which is rather more pronounced than normal.

There is an ethical problem here which I have been aware of for some time. It may be argued that students who have hypnosis to help them reduce their level of anxiety before an exam are gaining an unfair advantage over other students. This is the reason why I only help students who are experiencing a severe level of anxiety in relation to examinations. Nevertheless, one of the difficulties of using hypnosis in these sort of situations is that it may put other non-hypnotized individuals at a disadvantage, and this must be considered by all therapists who receive requests for this sort of help.

Gibbons (1979) also describes a number of uses of hypnosis in similar areas, such as achievement motivation, salesmanship, public speaking and foreign language study. There are a whole variety of other areas in which hypnosis may be of assistance, and some of these are discussed in more detail below.

CREATIVE BLOCKS

Nearly all creative individuals experience 'blocks' at some time. A creative block is simply a period in which the individual finds it impossible to carry out a creative task. This can happen to artists, writers, scientists, or to anyone involved in a creative ability. Many such individuals have particular strategies which they perform to attempt to get over this block. Creative blocks can have very serious consequences for the individual concerned. and can last for several months, or even years.

Barrios and Singer (1981) compared three different types of treatment for creative blocks. These were waking imagery, hypnotic dream, and rational discussion techniques. There was also a control group. Participants in the hypnotic dream condition experienced a hypnotic induction procedure and produced three hypnotic dreams related to their creative projects. There was no explicit mention of the term 'hypnosis', in case subjects' different expectations of hypnosis biased the results.

The results indicated that the hypnotic dream condition and the waking imagery condition were the most effective treatments for the creative blocks. This is an interesting use of hypnosis, and one which is likely to become more frequent, particularly as people with creative blocks realize that there are procedures available to help them.

CREATIVE EXPRESSION

Closely related to the treatment of creative blocks is the enhancement of creative expression. The essential difference is that in the former the person is unable to indulge in the creative ability at all, while in the latter the aim is to boost the creative process. This is an interesting area for the hypnotist to investigate. There are a whole variety of possibilities which can be explored.

For creators in the visual arts hypnosis may be of use in helping them visualize the next stage, or even the final stage, of their creation. Hypnosis may also be of general assistance in aiding concentration, and keeping attention focused on the task. Self-hypnosis may have a large role to play here. However, it is extremely difficult to provide convincing evidence that hypnosis is better than any other technique e.g. guided fantasy, since the area of creative expression does not lend itself well to measurement. Measuring the number of words written, or square inches painted, is hardly adequate. Despite these difficulties of measuring the effectiveness of hypnosis, if artists believe that their own creative process is being aided, then it warrants further investigation.

PERSONAL GROWTH

If each of us is honest, there will be certain areas in our personality which we would like to improve. These might be controlling a bad temper, improving social skills, or being less impulsive. As Gibbons (1979) points out, there have been a number of 'positive thinking' movements, probably the most well known being one of the earliest; Coue's (1932). In this people were instructed to repeat silently to themselves the words, 'Every day, and in every way, I am getting better and better'.

This was to be done during the period between sleep and wakefulness, when it was believed that the unconscious was more available to direct communication. There are always some people who are willing to attest to the effectiveness of these types of procedures, and attribute success in their lives to following these suggestions. However, they certainly do not have this effect for everybody, or indeed for the majority of people.

While such blanket uses of 'positive thinking' are rather naive, it should not be totally dismissed. If individuals can be given an appropriate belief that they are better in a particular area, they will probably feel happier as a result. Some people are actually performing well in a particular facet of their behaviour, but do not recognize this. The task here is not to change the person's behaviour, but to change their perception of this behaviour. In other words, to make them think more positively about it. Neurolinguistic programming attempts to do this by a process of reframing.

In cases where a person's perception of their own behaviour as inadequate is correct, then it is sensible to help them make their behaviour more adequate, and at the same time ensure that they think more positively about their behaviour. It is hard to produce lasting alterations in behaviour if individuals are still thinking about their behaviour as if it were inadequate.

While there is no doubt that many proponents of 'positive thinking' make exaggerated claims about its effectiveness, this should not blind therapists to the possibility that it has some useful applications. It should also be noted that it is generally pleasanter for an individual to have positive thoughts about their behaviour than to have negative thoughts.

SPORTS HYPNOSIS

This is an area in which there is now considerable interest. Sport is becoming more and more governed by commercial interests, and there is often tremendous pressure on individuals to perform at their peak. It must be stated clearly at the outset that there may be considerable danger in using hypnosis (or anything else) as an analgesic to enable someone to return to playing sport. Of course, it is not possible to say categorically that hypnosis should not be used for this purpose, for there are occasions when the cause of the pain is not aggravated by a return to playing sport, but great care should be taken in this respect.

It is the case in a number of sports that the team coach or captain often attempts to motivate the team. This is often referred to as 'psyching-up' the team. Shelton and Mahoney (1978) believe that there are four main aspects to the 'psyching-up' process. One emphasizes self-efficacy and personal ability, which may be described as ego-boosting. A second aspect is attentional focus, concentrating on the performance of certain muscles crucially involved in the performance of the sport. Preparatory arousal is the third aspect, where the sportsperson concentrates on being ready to start the event. The last aspect is imagery. Here the sportsperson concentrates on imagining themselves participating in the event (and doing well).

Richardson (1967a, 1967b) has reviewed the effects of mental practice, which is generally thought to be mental rehearsal of a particular physical action or group of actions in the absence of any gross muscular movements. He concludes that mental practice does improve performance in sports.

However Morgan (1980), in an examination of the uses of hypnosis in sports medicine, emphasizes that the effect of hypnosis may be extremely complex. It appears that there is little positive evidence that strength and endurance can be increased by hypnosis, although they may be decreased. One interesting finding is that exercise suggested under hypnosis does result in a change in various metabolic activities, such as heart rate, respiration rate, and oxygen uptake, which is similar to that which follows real exercise.

One possible use for this is in the warm-up procedure which most sportspersons go through. Although this may be vital in warming up cold muscles, where this is not so crucial, it might be that hypnotically suggested exercise provides a useful substitute. Morgan (1980) also suggests that it may be easier for some sportspersons to recognize their errors in performance under hypnosis than in their normal cognitive state.

Mairs (1984) reports a case study using hypnosis, in which the techniques used included mental practice, ego enhancement and attentional focus. The client wished to improve his archery scores, and after twelve sessions there were improvements in both his overall score and his grouping of arrows. He also reported that he was calmer and more relaxed in other aspects of his life. Archery lends itself particularly well to evaluation studies, as it is very measurement oriented, and an archer's performance is only indirectly affected by other competitors.

Udolf (1981) reports a case of a baseball player who used hypnosis to overcome his fear after being hit by the ball. It is important to remember that while hypnosis may be able to help sportspersons in various ways to improve their performance, it cannot give them abilities they do not possess. This is well illustrated by Udolf when he makes the point that making a boxer more aggressive may simply result in him getting hit more often.

From this brief review it can be seen that there are a number of possibilities which exist for the use of hypnosis in sport. However, it is certainly the case that these possibilities need a great deal of further investigation before they become any more than possibilities. For the investigator interested in this area, there are plenty of opportunities. In addition, in many sports measurement, e.g. time, distance, is very important. This opens the door to well-designed studies in which careful before and after measurements can be taken.

PERSONAL REFLECTIONS

I believe that it is in the non-clinical area that the greatest uses of self-hypnosis will be found. Leaving aside the view that in one sense all hypnosis is self-hypnosis, I would like to see individuals making use of self-hypnosis just as they make use of other strategies to help them 'cope' and grow personally.

While I am not an advocate of any particular 'personal growth' movement, I believe their aims are to be praised. However, I do not think that any one movement has a monopoly on the methods likely to achieve these aims. I would much rather see an individual given a whole variety of techniques which they can use when appropriate. Self-hypnosis should be one of those techniques.

Nor should extravagant claims be made of the benefits hypnosis can bring. As we have seen, the effectiveness of hypnosis in these areas has hardly begun to be measured. Unfortunately, there are always people around who will make excessive claims about the benefits of particular techniques. Even more unfortunately, there will always be people around who will believe them.

SELECTED READING

Gibbons, D. E. (1979) Applied Hypnosis and Hyperempiria, Plenum Press, New York

This book has an interesting chapter on the uses of hypnosis in improving creativity and performance. Although there is little empirical evidence, there are plenty of useful ideas for the therapist interested in this area.

Morgan, W. P. (1980) 'Hypnosis and Sports Medicine' in G. D. Burrows and L. Dennerstein (Eds.), <u>Handbook of Hypnosis and Psychosomatic Medicine</u>, Elsevier/North Holland Biomedical Press, Amsterdam

This is a very good review of the uses of hypnosis in sports medicine, and is particularly good at describing the complexities involved.

Chapter Nine

MISCELLANEOUS USES AND PROBLEMS OF HYPNOSIS

There are a number of other uses of hypnosis which have not been covered so far, and in this final chapter I will discuss some of these. It seems to me that these uses are much more likely to give rise to problems than the ones I have discussed in the previous two chapters. Consequently I wish to discuss a number of problems which have been associated with hypnosis, in an attempt to evaluate their seriousness.

PROBLEMS ASSOCIATED WITH HYPNOSIS

The problems associated with hypnosis reflect the multiplicity of its uses and the lack of knowledge about the nature of hypnosis. Some of the problems said to be associated with hypnosis result simply from misconceptions about it, some of which are perpetuated by the popular press. It is interesting to note that a person who is worried about being hypnotized will often raise a number of these problems.

Harmful Effects of Hypnosis
The question is often asked, 'Is hypnosis harmful?'. One is the possibility that hypnosis may lead to psychological or physical illness. This needs very careful consideration. It may be that some individuals experience physical or psychological problems after a hypnotic session. Hilgard, Hilgard and Newman (1961) reported that a small percentage of their subjects had headaches or other disturbances after being hypnotized. However, it could be that there is a problem of interpretation here.

A subject who is hypnotized may often feel 'different' after the session, even if no suggestions are given indicating this. It has been my experience that subjects have a variety of different physical and psychological feelings after hypnosis, and that the hypnotist has a crucial role in interpreting this for the subjects. Many subjects report they feel extremely relaxed after hypnosis, or even drowsy. It is quite possible that these feelings of drowsiness may be interpreted in some cases by the subjects as unpleasant. It is part of the job of the hypnotist in the debriefing following a hypnotic session to ensure that these feelings are correctly interpreted.

Similarly, it seems likely that at least some unpleasant physical sensations result from the subject maintaining the same body position throughout the session. These can include feelings of stiffness in muscles and temporary loss of kinaesthetic sensation. Again, it is the role of the hypnotist to brief the subjects about this possibility, so that they can correctly interpret the feelings.

There are also other possibilities that hypnotists need to be aware of. One is the possibility of producing physiological changes which might be dangerous to the subject. Morgan (1972) concluded that hypnotically suggested exercise was effective in altering the rate of some metabolic processes, such as heart rate, respiration rate and oxygen consumption. In fact, the metabolic rate resembles that produced by real exercise. For those subjects for whom exercise may prove dangerous, this type of suggestion is not to be recommended. Lockhart and Robertson (1977) reported a case of clinical tetany in one of their subjects, which fortunately they were able to deal with immediately.

The conclusion which I believe can be drawn from these findings is that unless there are good reasons to the contrary, instructions to subjects to alter their metabolic rate are best omitted. Although as far as I have been able to establish no death has resulted from any hypnotic suggestion, this does not mean that it is not a possibility. In fact Rosen (1960) has claimed that one patient committed suicide as a result of hypnotic removal of emotionally produced pain. Although it is far from clear that this hypnotic session was the causative agent, it is surely sensible for all hypnotists to do everything they can to ensure that no harm comes to their subjects or clients.

The question of whether hypnosis can be psychologically harmful is discussed very thoroughly by Udolf (1981). He is at pains to point out that the reports of psychological problems such as anxiety attacks, panic and depression being caused by hypnosis are much more frequent in clinical than experimental uses of hypnosis. There are a number of potential reasons for such problems, and for the differences between clinical and experimental settings. Many of these reasons, I believe, have their roots in the expectations of the subjects or clients.

In the clinical setting, the goal is to help the client. This may be done through hypnoanalysis, through hypnotically moderated behaviouristic techniques, or by some other method involving hypnosis. However, being in a clinical situation presupposes that the person has a problem. The fact that the person has a problem of some kind, whether a physical or psychological one, is likely to have an effect on their mental state. It seems to me that part of the reason why unpleasant psychological reactions are more likely in clinical settings is because the clients' problems adversely affect their psychological state.

Another possible reason for the differences is in the length of time for which the clients see their hypnotherapist, and the length of time for which the subjects see their hypnotist. I confess that I have no figures to back this up, but my impression from the literature is that typically the number of meetings for a client and hypnotherapist is many times that for a subject taking part in an experiment. It may be that the rapport which builds up is necessary before clients are prepared to reveal how they are feeling.

Clients are also likely to treat their hypnotherapists differently. It is much more appropriate to reveal feelings of depression and anxiety to a person who is attempting to help you with a particular problem. In fact clients are often explicitly questioned about their mental state. They have every right to expect help from their hypnotherapists, whereas subjects are much more likely to assume that help would not be forthcoming.

The techniques which are used in clinical and experimental settings differ, and it could be the case that this leads to some of the observed differences. There is also the possibility that some symptom substitution takes place, so that what looks like a panic attack, for example, is really the symptom manifesting itself in a different form.

One reason for psychological problems occurring in either clinical or experimental settings is that some individuals perceive the hypnotic session as a situation which is likely to give rise to rather strange feelings. Although hopefully most subjects who believe this are disabused about the idea, no doubt some still think this is likely to happen. It is hardly surprising if some individuals feel anxious or otherwise psychologically disturbed.

The point must also be made that simply being hypnotized is extremely unlikely to give rise to any unpleasant experiences. It is the phenomena which are suggested which result in unpleasant feelings, if such feelings occur. For instance, arm levitation may produce feelings of tiredness in the muscles in the arm, particularly if the procedure is prolonged, while suggesting that a part of the subject's body is growing hotter (or colder) may produce tingling sensations.

What final conclusions can be drawn about the dangers to the individual which may arise as a result of being hypnotized? Given the numbers of people who are hypnotized for experimental or clinical purposes every year, there are very few reports of psychological or physical problems, and those problems that are reported tend to be minor. It is not possible to ascertain what problems arise from visits to lay hypnotists, although one might expect more concern from the medical profession if they were continually having to deal with problems caused by visits to lay hypnotists. However, despite being treated by people with no real therapeutic skills, there seems little evidence that individuals come to any harm, except for having their bank balances considerably reduced!

The following four guidelines if followed by hypnotists would help ensure that the individuals they hypnotize do not have any problems. They are:

1. Find out what an individual's views about hypnosis are, and deal with any misconceptions.
2. Do not attempt to alter metabolic rate without knowledge of the person's medical background.
3. In clinical contexts, look for the meaning the symptom has for the client, and beware of symptom substitution.
4. Debrief adequately, in both clinical and experimental contexts.

So far we have assumed that the hypnotist has the best interests of the individual at heart, and has no intention of suggesting anything harmful. However, many members of the general public are worried that they might be asked to do something illegal or morally repulsive. Many experiments have tried to establish the extent to which this is possible.

One of the best known series of experiments is by Watkins (1947), who used highly susceptible subjects. These experiments fell into two categories, one in which the aim was to persuade the subjects to reveal secret information, while the aim of the other was to persuade the subjects to attack someone. In one experiment a message was given to some soldiers by their captain, and they were told not to disclose the message, either for financial reward, or because it was a military secret. They were then hypnotized, and told that their captain was present, and they were required to repeat the message to ensure it was correct. All did so, and also had amnesia for this disclosure.

One method by which subjects were induced to attack someone was by persuading them that the victim of their attack was an enemy. In perhaps the best known of these cases a soldier was convinced that his friend was in fact an enemy, and induced to attack him. Unfortunately, no-one knew that the soldier had a penknife, which he used to attack his friend. Apparently, serious injury was avoided only by the intervention of other people involved in the experiment.

These, and other studies, for example, Brenman (1942) and Young (1952), seem to indicate that some subjects can be persuaded under hypnosis to indulge in behaviour which is harmful either to themselves or others. However, a close analysis of the subjects' behaviours and motivations reveals that the situation is rather more complicated than it at first appears.

The most important factor seems to be the subjects' perception of the situation as an experimental one, as pointed out by Orne (1972). Once the situation is defined as an experimental one, then the subjects view it quite differently, and consequently behave differently. There are several factors determining their behaviour, and the relative weighting of these factors probably depends on the personality of the subject.

One factor is that the experimenter is perceived as 'responsible' for what happens. This is

153

often thought to mean that the experimenter has taken particular precautions to prevent the subject either being harmed, or causing harm to someone else, which is often the case. There is another dimension to this, which is that some subjects apparently expect the experimenter to take responsibility for their actions. In the work by Milgram (1969), the reactions of some subjects seemed to indicate that they believed they were inflicting real pain. Some of the subjects argued that they were only following orders, and consequently whatever happened was really the responsibility of the experimenter.

Another factor concerns the social demands of the situation. By agreeing to take part in the experiment the subject has entered into a contractual obligation with the experimenter, and may feel under strong social pressure to comply with the experimenter's demands. The obvious solution is to set up a situation in which the subjects are unaware they are taking part in an experiment. However, this is ethically unacceptable, and what some experimenters have done is to suggest behaviours which, although socially unacceptable, will supposedly not cause harm to the subjects or anyone else.

One such experiment was carried out by O'Brien and Rabuck (1976). This involved suggesting to female subjects that they attempt to make a date with a female confederate, in a situation it was hoped they would construe as homosexual. The subjects did this only in the waking state, and not post-hypnotically, or during hypnosis. Levitt, Overley and Rubinstein (1975) found that there was no significant difference between the number of subjects in a simulating group and a hypnotized group who were prepared to cut up an American flag or the Bible. These two experiments apparently demonstrate that there is nothing special about the hypnotic state when it comes to performing antisocial acts.

So far we have been looking at situations in which at least some ethical standards are in operation, but there are some cases where unscrupulous individuals have reputedly used hypnosis to aid them in committing criminal actions. Kline (1972) discusses two cases, one where an obstetrician used hypnotically induced fantasies to persuade patients to perform erotic acts with him, and the other where a graduate psychology student used hypnotically produced amnesia to cover up his sexual activities with young boys.

It would be an error, however, to consider hypnosis as the sole, or perhaps even the most important, factor in these cases. In a therapeutic relationship of any length, feelings of sexual attraction between the client and the therapist are far from unknown, and this could well explain how the obstetrician was able to seduce his clients. In the second case there are also a number of alternative explanations. The amnesia may not really have occurred at all, for unfortunately it is often the case that children who are sexually abused do not report such attacks anyway. Indeed even if amnesia did occur it may have been the attack itself which produced the amnesia, rather than the hypnotic suggestion.

The conclusion from all these studies is that there are generally factors in addition to the hypnosis itself which seem very powerful in bringing about the types of behaviour we have discussed. These include the relationship between the hypnotist and the subject, the degree to which the subjects believe that the experimenter takes responsibility for what occurs and will prevent them from harm, and the degree to which the social behaviour suggested is really seen as unacceptable by the subject. The final point is that as far as the honest professional is concerned, none of this is an issue anyway, although it is reassuring for individuals about to be hypnotized to know that they apparently suffer no greater risk as a result of being hypnotized.

FORENSIC HYPNOSIS

The main use of hypnosis within the area of forensics is to aid memory, although as Rowley (1984) has pointed out it may also be used to relax the witness, or to aid in determining the defendant's mental state. All of these uses are controversial, particularly the first, the use of hypnosis to aid the recollection of witnesses.

The use of hypnosis to aid memory has already been discussed in an earlier chapter, the general conclusion being that there is no convincing evidence to support the contention that hypnosis aids recall. Despite this, there have been a number of claims that hypnosis can enhance recall in criminal investigations, Haward and Ashworth (1980), Hibbard and Worring (1981) and Reiser and Nielson

(1980). However, two important review papers, Smith (1983) and Wagstaff (1984) both state that there is no clear evidence that hypnosis can aid memory recall, and also that hypnosis may lead to witnesses being more susceptible to leading questions.

This difference of opinion is usually attributable to the evidence considered by the two opposing groups. The group who support the use of hypnosis as a means of aiding recall in witnesses usually cite lots of individual cases and anecdotes, e.g. Kroger and Douce (1979). The more experimentally inclined reviewers look at the experimental literature, such as Putnam (1979), one of the first researchers to investigate scientifically the use of hypnosis in a context analogous to a forensic one.

The results so far appear quite conclusive. The cases cited in support of hypnotically enhanced recall of witnesses almost inevitably can be accounted for by other factors. These include the increased length of time for which questioning takes place, the perceived status of the hypnotist as an expert 'brought in' by the police, the tendency of hypnotized subjects to be more susceptible to leading questions and the possibility that the information was 'cued' by non-verbal signals unknowingly given by the interrogator.

The experimental evidence indicates very strongly that hypnosis has no positive effects on memory recall in subjects participating in experiments which set out to simulate real life situations. Indeed, a number seem to show that hypnosis may actually lead to less accurate recall, e.g. Wagstaff, Traverse and Milner (1982). Given this, the concern currently being expressed about the use of hypnosis in criminal cases supposedly to enhance witness recall is well motivated, and the decision by a number of supreme courts in the USA not to admit evidence from a witness who has undergone hypnosis is to be applauded.

The other two uses of hypnosis within the forensic context, although receiving much less discussion in the literature are no less controversial. The use of hypnosis to reduce anxiety in witnesses may give rise to the problems of accuracy of recall previously mentioned, and it may also, by making witnesses appear more relaxed and confident, make the jury more likely to believe their testimony. Similarly, the use of hypnosis to assist in determining the mental state of the defendant may give rise to the same problems of accuracy of recall. Rowley (1984) has concluded that hypnosis should not be used for either of these purposes.

Forensic hypnosis in many ways reflects much of what is worst about hypnosis in general. Outlandish claims have been made for it, with cases being miraculously solved, and what is more, some people who ought to know better appear to believe them. Given the lack of experimental evidence that hypnosis can aid recall, and the problems which can arise when it is used, there can be very few cases in which its use is justified.

MILITARY USES OF HYPNOSIS

Udolf (1981) makes the point that the use of hypnosis by the military is likely to be kept very secret. However, from the discussion which has taken place so far, few potential uses suggest themselves. The obvious one is the clinical use of hypnosis, particularly the relief of pain. The previous discussions have already pointed out the problems in areas such as interrogation and amnesia, two obvious military uses.

MOCK AUCTIONS

Mock auctions are peculiar occasions in which individuals apparently buy goods they do not want. Gibson (1977) gives a fascinating description of one of these. According to his account the seller uses a particular verbal form, very similar to a hypnotic induction procedure, to induce a hypnotic trance in some members of the audience, who as a result buy goods at hugely inflated prices.

However, it is not really necessary to invoke a hypnotic trance to explain this behaviour, for although it is probably the suggestible members of the audience who buy, it does not seem very parsimonious to invoke hypnosis to explain this, for many people are persuaded to do things they are apparently unwilling to do without being hypnotized. Despite this, Gibson's account is so compelling that one can hardly resist the temptation to investigate further.

STAGE HYPNOSIS

It is unfortunate that many people's experience of hypnosis is based solely on stage hypnosis, for not only does it give them a false impression of hypnosis, it may also make them more reluctant to accept therapeutic techniques involving hypnosis. However, few countries have laws regulating the use of stage hypnosis, and the stage hypnotist generally has complete freedom to persuade people to make fools of themselves.

A typical act might involve hallucinations, such as persuading people that they could eat a lemon, which would not taste bitter, but sweet like an orange. It might also involve age regression, and even regression to previous lives. A person might also be asked to imagine being a dog, and told to act like one. Sometimes people are also asked to perform feats of strength, and demonstrate insensitivity to pain. Post-hypnotic suggestions are also quite common. In short, they are asked to do things which the stage hypnotist believes the audience will find amusing.

However, it is far from clear that the majority of individuals who find their way up onto the stage are actually hypnotized, although a few may be. The beginning of the stage hypnotist's show usually involves asking the audience to perform an informal susceptibility test, such as the hand clasp test. A subset of the audience who demonstrate susceptibility on this test are then invited onto the stage.

The stage hypnotist then goes through an induction procedure, and the show is set to begin, but whether the people on stage are really hypnotized is another matter. The stage hypnotist is skilled at making things look impressive, but the people's behaviours can be accounted for in a different way. It is often said that people would not make such fools of themselves unless they really were hypnotized, but that is totally to misunderstand the situation.

Firstly, people do make fools of themselves without being hypnotized. Secondly, for people who wish to show off and do outrageous things, this provides a marvellous excuse to do so. Third, and perhaps most important, once the person is on the stage, tremendous social demands are operating. The expectations of the audience, the hypnotist, and the other people on the stage, are for the person to comply with the suggestions made. The question must be asked; 'Does the person feel more of a fool when he or she complies with the suggestion, or when he or she simply stands there looking embarrassed and feeling a failure because nothing is happening?' In these circumstances my guess would be that complying with the demands appears less ridiculous than not doing so.

I personally do not find it very entertaining to see people being persuaded to make fools of themselves, but I recognize that this is not sufficient reason for stage hypnosis to be banned. Paradoxically, although the idea is to persuade the audience that hypnosis is a mysterious state in which people can be made to do all manner of things, if this were really the case then hypnosis would quickly be recognized as too dangerous to be used as a stage act. Despite this, there may well be some unpleasant phenomena associated with stage hypnosis.

As I have indicated above, before a person is hypnotized, a few preliminary questions about their health are in order, since suggested physiological changes may bring about changes in metabolic rate, which could prove harmful to persons suffering from heart problems, asthma, etc. A number of the things which people are requested to do may also have unpleasant after effects, e.g. eating a lemon. Perhaps most worrying of all, people are sometimes required to imagine and act out events which occurred when they were younger. Some of these events are very distressing for the individual concerned, and if such emotional reactions arose in a clinical or experimental setting one would expect appropriate help to be forthcoming, whereas onstage the usual reaction is laughter. This seems to me a terrible invasion of privacy, and a complete disregard for human dignity.

The stage hypnotist, of course, has no skill in dealing with these problems, and there is no doubt that acts which involve people experiencing extreme emotional reactions, which are then laughed at, are at best totally unethical, and at worst harmful and very distressing. Some stage hypnotists attempt to induce phobic reactions in some members of the audience, a practice which is totally abhorrent. As something for people to ponder about, I would like to relate a particular event which happened several years ago.

A group of students attended a show in which a a stage hypnotist was performing, and after the usual susceptibility test, one of them was invited to take part in the show, and duly underwent an induction procedure. Part of the act involved regression to a previous life. Despite the complete ridiculousness of this suggestion, the student proceeded to describe a 'previous life' in which she was a nurse. The hypnotist asked her some questions about her age, and what year it was, and from her answers it was apparent that she had died in her twenties. The hypnotist asked her how she had died, and the student replied that she had committed suicide by taking a drug overdose.

The student was very distressed about this, not only at the time, but for some weeks afterwards. There are two very important factors to consider here. First, it is to be hoped that unless there was a strong therapeutic reason for pursuing this line of questioning, which is hard to believe, no professional hypnotist would ever do so. Second, if the person revealed such information spontaneously, then it is to be expected that a professional hypnotist would realize the importance of this particular statement. This incident has a very sad ending; some years after she finished her course the person committed suicide, death being caused by inhalation of carbon monoxide fumes. Coincidentally, the nurse, who she had claimed on stage was an earlier incarnation had been the same age when she died.

I think it is very clear that stage hypnosis may have unpleasant consequences for some individuals. Furthermore it is not possible for the stage hypnotist to identify these individuals in advance. For these reasons I believe that stage hypnosis should be regulated much more closely, or perhaps even banned altogether.

PERSONAL REFLECTIONS

For the professional who uses hypnosis in a responsible fashion, few problems are likely to arise. Even where hypnosis has been used in attempts to make people do unethical or injurious acts, it seems that the extent to which people perform these acts is determined by other factors, such as their view of the situation as an experimental one, and their relationship with the hypnotist.

However, if hypnosis is used carelessly, for instance if it is suggested to people who have been hypnotized that they relive an unpleasant event, or talk about something which is upsetting to them, they may suffer considerable psychological pain. If this is within a therapeutic context, then the means may be at hand to help alleviate this pain, but if this happens outside a professional setting, the person may experience considerable suffering.

Until much more is known about hypnosis, and the conditions under which various hypnotic phenomena occur, it is unlikely that many uses of hypnosis, for instance within the field of forensics, will prove effective. In our present state of knowledge it is premature to expect applications of hypnosis to show much success.

SELECTED READING

Gibson, H. B. (1977) Hypnosis: Its Nature and Therapeutic Uses, Peter Owen, London
This book contains an interesting discussion of harmful and criminal uses of hypnosis, and also of such phenomena as mock auctions.

Udolf, R. (1981) Handbook of Hypnosis for Professionals, Van Nostrand Reinhold Company, New York
Udolf's book contains a very thorough review of problems associated with hypnosis.

REFERENCES

Alladin, S. A. (1984) 'Hypnosis in the Treatment of
    Head Pain', Proceedings of the First Annual
    Conference of the British Society of
    Experimental and Clinical Hypnosis, pp. 12-34
Ambrose, G. (1952) 'Nervous Control of Sweating',
    Lancet, 1, 926
Ament, P. (1971) 'Removal of Gagging, a Response to
    Variable Behaviour Patterns', International
    Journal of Clinical and Experimental Hypnosis,
    39, 1-9
Anastasi, A. (1982) Psychological Testing (5th.
    ed.), Collier Macmillan Publishers, London
Araoz, D. L. (1982) Hypnosis and Sex Therapy,
    Brunner/Mazel, New York
August, R. V. (1961) Hypnosis in Obstetrics, McGraw-
    Hill, New York
Bakal, D. A. (1975) 'Headache: A Biopsychological
    Perspective', Psychological Bulletin, 82,
    369-82
Bakan, P. (1969) 'Hypnotizability, Laterality of Eye
    Movements and Functional Brain Asymmetry',
    Perceptual and Motor Skills, 28, 927-32
Banyai, E. I. and Hilgard, E. R. (1976) 'A
    Comparison of Active-Alert Hypnotic Induction
    with Traditional Relaxation Induction', Journal
    of Abnormal Psychology, 85, 218-24
Banyai, E. I., Meszaros, I. and Greguss, A. C.
    (1981) 'Alteration of Activity Level: The
    Essence of Hypnosis or a Byproduct of the Type
    of Induction?' in G. Adam, I. Meszaros and E.
    I. Banyai (eds.), Brain and Behaviour, vol.
    17, Pergamon Press, Budapest, Hungary
Barabasz, A. F. (1977) New Techniques in Behavior
    Therapy and Hypnosis, Power Publishers Inc.,
    South Orange, New Jersey
Barber, T. X. (1962) 'Hypnotic Age Regression: a
    Critical Review', Psychosomatic Medicine, 24,
    286-99
Barber, T. X. (1964) 'Hypnotizability,
    Suggestibility and Personality: a Critical
    Review of Research Findings', Psychological
    Reports, Monograph Supplement, 14, 299-320

Barber, T. X. (1965) 'Measuring "Hypnotic-like"
Suggestibility with and without "Hypnotic
Induction"; Psychometric Properties, Norms, and
Variables Influencing Response to the Barber
Suggestibility Scale (BSS)', Psychological
Reports, 16, 809-44

Barber, T. X. (1969) Hypnosis: A Scientific
Approach, Van Nostrand-Reinhold Company, New
York

Barber, T. X. (1972) 'Suggested ("Hypnotic")
Behavior: The Trance Paradigm Versus an
Alternative Paradigm', in E. Fromm and R. E.
Shor (eds.), Hypnosis: Research Developments
and Perspectives, Aldine-Atherton, Chicago, pp.
115-82

Barber, T. X. (1979) 'Suggested ("Hypnotic")
Behaviour: The Trance Paradigm Versus an
Alternative Paradigm', in E. Fromm and R. E.
Shor (eds.), Hypnosis: Developments in Research
and New Perspectives, Aldine Publishing
Company, New York, pp. 217-71

Barber, T. X. and Calverley, D. S. (1962) '"Hypnotic
Behavior" as a Function of Task Motivation',
Journal of Psychology, 54, 363-89

Barber, T. X. and Calverley, D. S. (1964) 'Towards a
Theory of "Hypnotic" Behavior: An Experimental
Study of "Hypnotic" Time Distortion', Archives
of General Psychiatry, 10, 209-16

Barber, T. X. and Ham, M. W. (1974) Hypnotic
Phenomena, General Learning Press, Morristown,
New Jersey

Barber, T. X. and Wilson, S. C. (1977) 'Hypnosis,
Suggestions, and Altered States of
Consciousness: Experimental Evaluation of the
New Cognitive-Behavioral Theory and the
Traditional Trance-State Theory of "Hypnosis"',
in W. E. Edmonston, Jr. (ed.), Conceptual and
Investigative Approaches to Hypnosis and
Hypnotic Phenomena, Annals of the New York
Academy of Sciences, 296, pp. 34-47

Barrios, M. V. and Singer, J. L. (1981) 'The
Treatment of Creative Blocks: A Comparison of
Waking Imagery, Hypnotic Dream, and Rational
Discussion Techniques', Imagination, Cognition
and Personality, 1, 89-109

Baumann, F. (1970) 'Hypnosis and the Adolescent Drug
Abuser', The American Journal of Clinical
Hypnosis, 13, 17-21

Benson, H. and Klipper, M. Z. (1976) The Relaxation
Response, Collins, London

Benson, H., Kotch, J. B., Crassweller, K. D. and
Greenwood, M. (1977) 'Historical and Clinical
Considerations of the Relaxation Response',
American Scientist, 65, 441-45
Birkett, P. (1979) 'Relationships Among Handedness,
Familial Handedness, Sex and Ocular Sighting
Dominance', Neuropsychologia, 17, 533-37
Bowers, K. S. (1967) 'The Effects of Demands for
Honesty on Reports of Visual and Auditory
Hallucinations', International Journal of
Clinical and Experimental Hypnosis, 15, 31-36
Bowers, K. S. (1976) Hypnosis for the Seriously
Curious, Brooks/Cole Publishing Company,
Monterey, California
Bowers, K. S. (1979) 'Time Distortion and Hypnotic
Ability: Underestimating the Duration of
Hypnosis', Journal of Abnormal Psychology, 88,
435-39
Bowers, K. S. (1981) 'Has the Sun Set on the
Stanford Scales?', The American Journal of
Clinical Hypnosis, 2, 79-88
Bowers, K. S. and Brenneman, H. A. (1979) 'Hypnosis
and the Perception of Time', International
Journal of Clinical and Experimental Hypnosis,
27, 29-41
Braid, J. (1846) The Power of the Mind Over the
Body, John Churchill, London
Brenman, M. (1942) 'Experiments in the Hypnotic
Production of Anti-social and Self-injurious
Behavior', Psychiatry, 5, 49-61
Brenneman, H. A. (1978) 'Peer Descriptions During
Hypnotic Age Regression', Paper Presented at
the 30th. Annual Meeting of the Society for
Clinical and Experimental Hypnosis, Ashville,
North Carolina
Broadbent, D. E. (1957) 'A Mechanical Model for
Human Attention and Immediate Memory',
Psychological Review, 64, 205-15
Browning, C. W. and Crasilneck, H. B. (1957) 'The
Experimental Use of Hypnosis in Suppression
Amblyopia', The American Journal of Opthalmology
44, 468
Browning, C. W., Quinn, L. H. and Crasilneck, H. B.
(1958), 'The Use of Hypnosis in Suppressing
Amblyopia of Children', The American Journal of
Opthalmology, 46, 53-67
Budzynski, T. H. (1979) 'Biofeedback Strategies in
Headache Treatment', in J. V. Basmajian (ed.),
Biofeedback: A Handbook for Clinicians, Williams
and Wilkins, Baltimore

Byrne, R. (1983) 'Protocol Analysis in Problem
    Solving', in J. St. B. T. Evans (ed.), Thinking
    and Reasoning: Psychological Approaches,
    Routledge and Kegan Paul, London, pp. 227-49
Casey, K. L. (1970) 'Some Current Views on the
    Neurophysiology of Pain', in Crue, B. L. (ed.),
    Pain and Suffering, Thomas, Springfield,
    Illinois, pp. 168-75
Casey, K. L. (1973) 'Pain: a Current View of Neural
    Mechanisms', American Scientist, 61, 194-200
Cautela, J. R. (1966) 'Treatment of Compulsive
    Behaviour by Covert Sensitisation', The
    Psychological Record, 16, 33-41
Cautela, J. R. (1967) 'Covert Sensitisation'
    Psychological Reports, 20, 459-68
Cautela, J. R. (1975) 'The Use of Covert
    Conditioning in Hypnotherapy', International
    Journal of Clinical and Experimental Hypnosis,
    23, 15-27
Chertok, L. and Kramarz, P. (1959) 'Hypnosis, Sleep,
    and Electro-encephalography', Journal of
    Nervous and Mental Disease, 128, 227-38
Chiasson, S. W. (1964) 'Hypnosis in Postoperative
    Urinary Retention' American Journal of Clinical
    Hypnosis, 7, 366-68
Collison, D. R. (1975) 'Which Asthmatic Patients
    Should be Treated by Hypnotherapy?' Medical
    Journal of Australia, 1, 776-81
Cooper, L. F. and Erickson, M. H. (1959) Time
    Distortion in Hypnosis, (2nd. ed.), Williams
    and Wilkins, Baltimore
Cooper, L. F. and Erickson, M. H. (1980) 'Time
    Distortion in Hypnosis: II', in E. L. Rossi.
    (ed.), The Collected Papers of Milton H.
    Erickson on Hypnosis, vol. II: Hypnotic
    Alteration of Sensory, Perceptual and
    Physiological Processes, Irvington, New York
Cooper, L. M. and London, P. (1973) 'Reactivation of
    Memory by Hypnosis and Suggestion',
    International Journal of Clinical and
    Experimental Hypnosis, 21, 312-23
Cornwell, J., Burrows, G. D. and McMurray, N. (1981)
    'Comparison of Single and Multiple Sessions of
    Hypnosis in the Treatment of Smoking
    Behaviour', Australian Journal of Clinical and
    Experimental Hypnosis, 9, 61-76
Coue, E. (1922) Self-mastery Through Conscious
    Autosuggestion, Allen and Unwin, London

Cowell, D. and Franklin, J. (1983) 'The Use of
    Progressive Relaxation and Hypnosis in
    Counselling Secondary School Pupils', British
    Journal of Guidance and Counselling, 11, 160-
    69
Crasilneck, H. B. and Hall, J. A. (1975) Clinical
    Hypnosis: Principles and Practice, Grune and
    Stratton, New York
Daniels, L. K. (1976) 'Rapid In-office and In-vivo
    Desensitization of an Injection Phobia
    Utilizing Hypnosis', American Journal of
    Clinical Hypnosis, 18, 200-203
Degun, M. D. and Degun, G. (1982) 'The Use of
    Hypnosis in the Treatment of Psychosexual
    Disorders: With Case Illustrations of
    Vaginismus', Bulletin of the British Society of
    Experimental and Clinical Hypnosis, 5, 31-36
Degun, M. D. and Degun, G. (1983) 'Covert
    Sensitisation with the Use of Hypnosis',
    British Journal of Experimental and Clinical
    Hypnosis, 1, 27-32
Delprato, D. J. and Holmes, P. A. (1978)
    'Facilitation of Arm Levitation by Responses to
    Previous Suggestions of a Different Type',
    International Journal of Clinical and
    Experimental Hypnosis, 26, 167-77
Dement, W. C. and Kleitman, N. (1957) 'Cyclic
    Variations in EEG During Sleep and their
    Relations to Eye Movement, Body Motility, and
    Dreaming, EEG Clinical Neurophysiology, 9, 673-
    90
Dengrove, E. (1973) 'The Uses of Hypnosis in
    Behavior Therapy', International Journal of
    Clinical and Experimental Hypnosis, 21, 13-17
Dhanens, T. P. and Lundy, R. M. (1975) 'Hypnotic and
    Waking Suggestions and Recall', International
    Journal of Clinical and Experimental Hypnosis,
    23, 68-79
Diamond, M. J. (1982) 'Modifying Hypnotic
    Experiences by Means of Indirect Hypnosis and
    Hypnotic Skill Training: an Update (1981),
    Research Communications in Psychology,
    Psychiatry and Behaviour, 7, 233-39
Diment, A. D. (1981) 'A Use of Hypnosis in a Case of
    Barbiturate Dependence', Australian Journal of
    Clinical and Experimental Hypnosis, 9, 101-5
Edmonston, W. E., Jr. (1981) Hypnosis and
    Relaxation: Modern Verification of an Old
    Equation, John Wiley and Sons, Chichester

Ehrenreich, G. A. (1963) 'The Influence of
Unconscious Factors on Hypnotizability' in M.
V. Kline (ed.), Clinical Correlates of
Experimental Hypnosis, Thomas, Illinois, pp.
136-51
Epstein, W. (1972) 'Mechanisms of Directed
Forgetting', in G. H. Bower (ed.), The Psychology
of Learning and Motivation, vol. 6, Academic
Press, New York
Ericsson, K. A. and Simon, H. A. (1980) 'Verbal
Reports as Data', Psychological Review, 87,
215-51
Erickson, M. H. (1938) 'A Study of Clinical and
Experimental Findings on Hypnotic Deafness: II
Experimental Findings with a Conditioned
Response Technique', Journal of General
Psychology, 19, 151-67
Erickson, M. H. (1939) 'The Induction of Color-
Blindness by a Technique of Hypnotic Suggestion',
Journal of General Psychology, 20, 61-69
Erickson, M. H. (1954) 'Special Techniques of Brief
Hypnotherapy', Journal of Clinical and
Experimental Hypnosis, 2, 109
Erickson, M. H. (1958) 'Naturalistic Techniques of
Hypnosis', American Journal of Clinical
Hypnosis, 1, 3-8
Erickson, M. H. (1964) 'Pantomime Techniques in
Hypnosis and the Implications', American
Journal of Clinical Hypnosis, 7, 64-70
Erickson, M. H., Herschman, S. and Secter, I. I.
(1961) The Practical Application of Medical
and Dental Hypnosis, Julian Press, New York
Erickson, M. H., Rossi, E. L. and Rossi, S. (1976)
Hypnotic Realities. The Induction of Clinical
Hypnosis and Forms of Indirect Suggestion,
Irvington Press: New York
Esdaile, J. (1850) Mesmerism in India and its
Practical Application in Surgery and Medicine,
Longman's, Green and Company, London
Evans, F. J. (1979) 'Hypnosis and Sleep: Techniques
for Exploring Cognitive Activity During Sleep',
in E. Fromm and R. E. Shor (eds.), Hypnosis:
Developments in Research and New Developments,
Aldine Publishing Company, New York, pp. 139-83
Evans, F. J. (1982) 'Hypnosis and Sleep', Research
Communications in Psychology, Psychiatry and
Behavior, 7, 241-56

Evans, F. J. and Orne, M. T. (1971) 'The
    Disappearing Hypnotist: The Use of Stimulating
    Subjects to Evaluate How Subjects Perceive
    Experimental Procedures', International Journal
    of Clinical and Experimental Hypnosis, 19, 277-
    96
Eysenck, H. J. and Furneaux, W. D. (1945) 'Primary
    and Secondary Suggestibility: An Experimental
    and Statistical Study', Journal of Experimental
    Psychology, 35, 485-503
Fee, A. F. and Reilley, R. R. (1982) 'Hypnosis in
    Obstetrics: A Review of Techniques', Journal of
    the American Society of Psychosomatic Dentistry
    and Medicine, 29, 17-29
Fellows, B. J. (1979) 'The British Use of the Barber
    Suggestibility Scale: Norms, Psychometric
    Properties and the Effects of the Sex of the
    Subject and of the Experimenter', British
    Journal of Psychology, 70, 547-57
Fellows, B. J. (1982) 'Review of G. F. Wagstaff's
    "Hypnosis, Compliance and Belief", The
    Harvester Press, Brighton', Bulletin of the
    British Society of Experimental and Clinical
    Hypnosis, 5, 61-65
Fellows, B. J. (1984) 'Hypnosis Research in
    Hungary', British Journal of Experimental and
    Clinical Hypnosis, 1, 29-34
Fellows, B. J. and Creamer, M. (1978) 'An
    Investigation of the Role of 'Hypnosis',
    Hypnotic Susceptibility and Hypnotic Induction
    in the Production of Age Regression', British
    Journal of Social and Clinical Psychology, 17,
    165-71
Fewtrell, W. D. (1984) 'Psychological Approaches to
    Panic Attack - Some Recent Developments', British
    Journal of Experimental and Clinical Hypnosis,
    1, 21-24
French, N. (1984) Successful Hypnotherapy, Thorsons
    Publishers Ltd., Wellingborough
Frischholz, E,J. and Spiegel, D. (1983) 'Hypnosis Is
    Not Therapy', Bulletin of the British Society
    of Experimental and Clinical Hypnosis, 6, 3-8
Frischholz, E. J., Spiegel, D., Spiegel, H., Balma,
    D. L. and Markell, C. S. (1982) 'Differential
    Hypnotic Responsivity of Smokers, Phobics, and
    Chronic-Pain Control Patients: a Failure to
    Confirm', Journal of Abnormal Psychology, 91,
    269-72

Frischholz, E. J., Spiegel, H., Tryon, W. W. and
    Fisher, S. (1981) 'The Relationship between the
    Hypnotic Induction Profile and the Stanford
    Hypnotic Susceptibility Scale, Form C:
    Revisited', The American Journal of Clinical
    Hypnosis, 24, 98-104
Frischholz, E. J., Tryon, W. W., Vellios, A. T.,
    Fisher, S., Maruffi, B. L. and Spiegel, H.
    (1980) 'The Relationship between the Hypnotic
    Induction Profile and the Stanford Hypnotic
    Susceptibility Scale, Form C: a Replication',
    American Journal of Clinical Hypnosis, 22, 185-
    96
Fromm, E. (1975) 'Self hypnosis: A New Area of
    Research', Psychotherapy: Research, Theory and
    Practice, 12, 295-301
Fromm, E. (1979) 'The Nature of Hypnosis and Other
    Altered States of Consciousness: An Ego-
    Psychological Theory', in E. Fromm and R. E.
    Shor (eds.), Hypnosis: Developments in Research
    and New Perspectives, Aldine Publishing
    Company, New York, pp. 81-103
Frumkin, L. R., Ripley, H. S. and Cox, G. B. (1978)
    'Changes in Cerebral Hemispheric Lateralization
    with Hypnosis', Biological Psychiatry, 13, 741-
    50
Furneaux, W. D. and Chapple, P. A. L. (1964) 'Some
    Objective and Subjective Characteristics of
    Labor Influenced by Personality, and their
    Modification by Hypnosis and Relaxation',
    Proceedings of the Royal Society of Medicine,
    57, 261-62
Gardner, G. G. and Olness, K. (1981) Hypnosis and
    Hypnotherapy with Children, Grune and Stratton,
    New York
Gerschman, J. A., Burrows, G. D. and Fitzgerald, P.
    J. (1981) 'Hypnosis in the Control of Gagging',
    Australian Journal of Clinical and Experimental
    Hypnosis, 9, 53-59
Gibbons, D. E. (1979) Applied Hypnosis and
    Hyperempiria, Plenum Press, New York
Gibson, H. B. (1977) 'Hypnosis: Its Nature and
    Therapeutic Benefits', Peter Owen, London
Gibson, H. B. (1981) 'Review of S. R. Smith "A
    Primer of Hypnosis", British Society of Medical
    and Dental Hypnosis, Ashstead, Surrey',
    Bulletin of the British Society of Experimental
    and Clinical Hypnosis, 4, 32

References

Gibson, H. B. (1983) 'A Comment on Frischholz and
    Spiegel's "Hypnosis is not Therapy"', Bulletin
    of the British Society of Experimental and
    Clinical Hypnosis, 6, 9-13
Gibson, H. B. (1984) 'The Treatment of Pain by
    Hypnotic Techniques', Proceedings of the First
    Annual Conference of the British Society of
    Experimental and Clinical Hypnosis, pp. 34-45
Gibson, H. B. and Corcoran, M. E. (1975)
    'Personality and Differential Susceptibility to
    Hypnosis: Further Replication and Sex
    Differences', British Journal of Psychology,
    66, 513-20
Gibson, H. B. and Curran, J. D. (1974) 'Hypnotic
    Susceptibility and Personality: a Replication
    Study', British Journal of Psychology, 65, 283-
    91
Gill, M. M. and Brenman, M. (1959) Hypnosis and
    Related States: Psychoanalytic Studies in
    Regression, International Universities Press,
    New York
Grabowska, M. J. (1971) 'The Effect of Hypnosis and
    Hypnotic Suggestion on the Blood Flow in the
    Extremities', Polish Medical Journal, 10,
    1044-51
Gruenewald, D. (1982) 'A Psychoanalytic View of
    Clinical Hypnosis', The American Journal of
    Clinical Hypnosis, 24, 185-90
Gur, R. C. and Gur, R. E. (1974) 'Handedness, Sex
    and Eyedness as Moderating Variables in the
    Relation between Hypnotic Susceptibility and
    Functional Brain Asymmetry', Journal of
    Abnormal Psychology, 83, 635-43
Hart, B. B. (1984) 'Hypnotic Age Regression of
    Long-standing Phobia: Two Case Studies',
    Proceedings of the First Annual Conference of
    the British Society of Experimental and
    Clinical Hypnosis, pp. 54-60
Hartland, J. C. (1971) Medical and Dental Hypnosis,
    (2nd. ed.), Williams and Wilkins, Baltimore
Haward, L. R. C. and Ashworth, A. (1980) 'Some
    Problems of Evidence Obtained by Hypnosis',
    Criminal Law Review, August, 469-85
Hellier, F. F. (1951) 'The Treatment of Warts with
    X-rays. Is their Action Physical or
    Psychological?' British Journal of Dermatology,
    63, 193-94
Hempel, C. G. (1966) Philosophy of Natural Science,
    Prentice-Hall Inc., Englewood Cliffs, New
    Jersey

References

Hibbard, W. S. and Worring, R. W. (1981) <u>Forensic</u>
    <u>Hypnosis</u>, Thomas, Springfield, Illinois
Hilgard, E. R. (1965) <u>Hypnotic Susceptibility</u>,
    Harcourt, Brace and World, New York
Hilgard, E. R. (1968) <u>The Experience of Hypnosis</u>,
    Harcourt, Brace and World, New York
Hilgard, E. R. (1973a) 'Dissociation Revisited', in
    M. Henle, J. Jaynes and J. J. Sullivan (eds.),
    <u>Historical Conceptions of Psychology</u>, Springer,
    New York, pp. 205-19
Hilgard, E. R. (1973b) 'A Neodissociation Theory of
    Pain Reduction in Hypnosis', <u>Psychological</u>
    <u>Review</u>, <u>80</u>, 396-411
Hilgard, E. R. (1974) 'Towards a Neodissociation
    Theory: Multiple Cognitive Controls in Human
    Functioning', <u>Perspectives in Biological</u>
    <u>Medicine</u>, <u>17</u>, 301-16
Hilgard, E. R. (1975) 'Hypnosis' in M. R. Rosenzweig
    and L. W. Porter (eds.), <u>Annual Review of</u>
    <u>Psychology</u>, <u>26</u>, 19-44
Hilgard, E. R. (1981a) 'The Eye Roll Sign and Other
    Scores of the Hypnotic Induction Profile (HIP)
    as Related to the Stanford Hypnotic
    Susceptibility Scale, Form C (SHSS:C): a
    Critical Discussion of a Study by Frischholz
    and Others', <u>The American Journal of Clinical</u>
    <u>Hypnosis</u>, <u>24</u>, 89-97
Hilgard, E. R. (1981b) 'Further Discussion of the
    HIP and the Stanford Form C: a Reply to a Reply
    by Frischholz, Spiegel, Tryon and Fisher', <u>The</u>
    <u>American Journal of Clinical Hypnosis</u>, <u>24</u>,
    106-8
Hilgard, E. R. and Bentler, P. M. (1963) 'Predicting
    Hypnotizability from the Maudsley Personality
    Inventory', <u>British Journal of Psychology</u>, <u>54</u>,
    63-9
Hilgard, E. R. and Hilgard, J. R. (1983) <u>Hypnosis in</u>
    <u>the Relief of Pain</u> (rev. ed.), William
    Kaufmann Inc., Los Altos, California
Hilgard, E. R., Sheehan, P. W., Monteiro, K. P. and
    Macdonald, H. (1981) 'Factorial Structure of
    the Creative Imagination Scale as a Measure of
    Hypnotic Responsiveness: An International
    Comparative Study', <u>International Journal of</u>
    <u>Clinical and Experimental Hypnosis</u>, <u>29</u>, 66-76
Hilgard, J. R. (1979) 'Imaginative and Sensory-
    Affective Involvements in Everyday Life and in
    Hypnosis', in E. Fromm and R. E. Shor (eds.),
    <u>Hypnosis: Developments in Research and New</u>
    <u>Perspectives</u>, Aldine Publishing Company, New
    York, pp. 483-517

Hilgard, J. R., Hilgard, E. R. and Newman, M. F. (1961) 'Sequelae to Hypnotic Induction with Special Reference to Earlier Chemical Anaesthesia', Journal of Nervous and Mental Disease, 133, 461-478

Hilgard, J. R. and Morgan, A. H. (1978) 'Treatment of Anxiety and Pain in Childhood Cancer Through Hypnosis', in F. H. Frankel and H. S. Zamansky (eds.), Hypnosis at its Bicentennial: Selected Papers, Plenum Press, New York

Horsley, I. A. (1982) 'Hypnosis and Self-hypnosis in the Treatment of Psychogenic Dysphonia: A Case Report', American Journal of Clinical Hypnosis, 24, 277-283

Hull, C. L. (1933) Hypnosis and Suggestibility: An Experimental Approach, Appleton-Century-Crofts, New York

Humphrey, N. (1984) Consciousness Regained, Oxford University Press, Oxford

Jacobson, E. (1938) Progressive Relaxation, University of Chicago Press, Chicago

Jacobson, E. (1962) You Must Relax, McGraw-Hill, New York

Jaynes, J. (1976) The Origins of Consciousness in the Breakdown of the Bicameral Mind, Houghton-Mifflin, Boston

Johnson, R. F. Q. (1976) 'Hypnotic Time Distortion and the Enhancement of Learning: New Data Pertinent to the Krauss-Katzell-Krauss Experiment', American Journal of Clinical Hypnosis, 19, 98-102

Johnson, R. F. Q., Maher, B. A. and Barber, T.X. (197 'Artifact in the "Essence of Hypnosis": An Evaluation of Trance Logic', Journal of Abnormal and Social Psychology, 79, 212-20

Katz, N. W. (1979) 'Comparative Efficacy of Behavioral Training, Training Plus Relaxation, and a Sleep/Trance Hypnotic Induction in Increasing Hypnotic Susceptibility', Journal of Consulting and Clinical Psychology, 47, 119-27

Kent, G. (1986) 'Hypnosis in Dentistry', British Journal of Experimental and Clinical Hypnosis, 3, 103-112

Kline, M. V. (1953) 'Delimited Hypnotherapy: the Acceptance of Resistance in the Treatment of a Long-standing Neurodermatitis with a Sensory-imagery Technique', Journal of Clinical and Experimental Hypnosis, 1, 18

Kline, M. V. (1972) 'The Production of Antisocial Behavior Through Hypnosis: New Clinical Data', International Journal of Clinical and Experimental Hypnosis, 20, 80-94

Kraft, T. (1984) 'Injection Phobia: A Case Study', British Journal of Experimental and Clinical Hypnosis, 1, 13-18

Krauss, H. H., Katzell, R. and Krauss, B. J. (1974) 'Effect of Hypnotic Time Distortion Upon Free Recall Learning', Journal of Abnormal Psychology, 83, 140-44

Kroger, W. S. (1977) Clinical and Experimental Hypnosis in Medicine, Dentistry and Psychology, J. B. Lippincott Company, Philadelphia

Kroger, W. S. and Douce, R. G. (1979) 'Hypnosis in Criminal Investigation', International Journal of Clinical and Experimental Hypnosis, 27, 358-74

Kroger, W. S. and Fezler, W. D. (1976) Hypnosis and Behavior Modification: Imagery Conditioning, J. B. Lippincott Company, Philadelphia

Labaw, W., Holton, C., Tewell, K. and Eccles, D. (1975) 'The Use of Self-hypnosis by Children with Cancer', American Journal of Clinical Hypnosis, 17, 233-38

Laguaite, J. K. (1976) 'The Use of Hypnosis with Children with Deviant Voices', The International Journal of Clinical and Experimental Hypnosis, 24, 98-104

Lazar, B. S. (1977) 'Hypnotic Imagery as a Tool in Working with a Cerebral Palsied Child', The International Journal of Clinical and Experimental Hypnosis', 25, 78-87

Lazarus, A. A. (1971) Behavior Therapy and Beyond, McGraw-Hill, New York

LeCron, L. M. and Bordeaux, J. (1949) Hypnotism Today, Grune and Stratton, New York

Levitt, E. E., Overley, T. M. and Rubinstein, D. (1975) 'The Objectionable Act as a Mechanism for Testing the Coercive Power of the Hypnotic State', American Journal of Clinical Hypnosis, 17, 263-66

Lockhart, R. S. and Robertson, A. W. (1977) 'Hypnosis and Speech Therapy as a Combined Therapeutic Approach to the Problem of Stammering', British Journal of Disorders of Communication, 12, 97-108

London, P. (1963) Children's Hypnotic Susceptibility Scale, Consulting Psychologists Press, Palo Alto, California

London, P. (1965) 'Developmental Experiments in Hypnosis', Journal of Projective Techniques and Personality Assessment, 29, 189-99

Ludwig, A. M. (1969) 'Altered States of Consciousness' in C. T. Tart (ed.), Altered States of Consciousness, John Wiley and Sons Inc., New York, pp. 9-22

Maher-Loughnan, G. P. (1970) 'Hypnosis and Auto-hypnosis for the Treatment of Asthma', International Journal of Clinical and Experimental Hypnosis, 18, 1-14

Mairs, D. A. E. (1984) 'Hypnosis in Sport: a Case Study', in Proceedings of the First Annual Conference of the British Society of Experimental and Clinical Hypnosis, pp. 178-186

Mason, C. F. (1961) 'Hypnotic Motivation of Aphasics', International Journal of Clinical and Experimental Hypnosis, 9, 297-301

Maupin, E. W. (1969) 'On Meditation' in C. T. Tart (ed.), Altered States of Consciousness, John Wiley and Sons Inc., New York, pp. 177-186

McCue, P. A. (1982) 'Hypnotic Time Distortion: Experimental Work, Clinical Applications and Theoretical Considerations', Bulletin of the British Society of Experimental and Clinical Hypnosis, 5, 14-20

McCue, P. A. (1983) 'A Comment on Frischholz and Spiegel's "Hypnosis is not Therapy"', Bulletin of the British Society of Experimental and Clinical Hypnosis, 6, 19-21

McDonald, R. D. and Smith, J. R. (1975) 'Trance Logic in Tranceable and Simulating Subjects', Journal of Clinical and Experimental Hypnosis, 23, 80-89

Melei, J. and Hilgard, E. R. (1964) 'Attitudes Towards Hypnosis Self Predictions and Hypnotic Susceptibility', International Journal of Clinical and Experimental Hypnosis, 12, 99-108

Melzack, R., and Wall, P. D. (1965) 'Pain Mechanisms: A New Theory', Science, 150, 971-79

Milgram, S. (1969) Obedience to Authority, Harper and Row Publishers Inc., New York

Miller, M. M. (1979) Therapeutic Hypnosis, Human Sciences Press, New York

Mischel, W. (1968) Personality and Assessment, Wiley, New York

Mitchell, R. (1982) Phobias, Penguin, Harmondsworth

Moon, T. and Moon, H. (1984) 'Hypnosis and Childbirth: Self-report and Comment', British Journal of Experimental and Clinical Hypnosis, 1, 49-52

Morgan, A. H. (1973) 'The Heritability of Hypnotic Susceptibility in Twins', Journal of Abnormal Psychology, 82, 55-61

Morgan, A. H. and Hilgard, E. R. (1973) 'Age Differences in Susceptibility', International Journal of Abnormal Psychology, 82, 55-61

Morgan, A. H. and Hilgard, E. R. (1979) 'The Stanford Hypnotic Clinical Scale for Children', The American Journal of Clinical Hypnosis, 21, 148-55

Morgan, A. H., Johnson, D. L. and Hilgard, E. R. (1974) 'The Stability of Hypnotic Susceptibility: A Longitudinal Study', International Journal of Clinical and Experimental Hypnosis, 22, 249-57

Morgan, A. H., MacDonald, H. and Hilgard, E. R. (1974) 'EEG Alpha: Lateral Asymmetry Related to Task and Hypnotisability', Psychophysiology, 11, 275-82

Morgan, W. P. (1972) 'Hypnosis and Muscular Performance' in W. P. Morgan (ed.), Erogenic Aids and Muscular Performance, Academic Press, New York

Morgan, W. P. (1980) 'Hypnosis in Sports Medicine', in G. D. Burrows and L. Dennerstein (Eds.), Handbook of Hypnosis and Psychosomatic Medicine, Elsevier/North Holland Biomedical Press, New York

Moss, A. A. (1977) 'Hypnodontics: Hypnosis in Dentistry', in W. S. Kroger, Clinical and Experimental Hypnosis, J. B. Lippincott, Philadelphia

Oatley, K. (1981) 'Representing Ourselves: Mental Schemata, Computational Metaphors, and the Nature of Consciousness', in G. Underwood and R. Stevens (eds.), Aspects of Consciousness: vol 2, Structural Issues, Academic Press, London

O'Brien, R. M. and Rabuck, S. J. (1976) 'Experimentally Produced Self-repugnant Behavior as a Function of Hypnosis and Waking Suggestion: a Pilot Study', American Journal of Clinical Hypnosis, 18, 272-76

Olness, K. (1981) 'Imagery (Self-hypnosis) as Adjunct Therapy in Childhood Cancer', American Journal of Pediatric Hematology/Oncology, 3, 313-21

Orne, M. T. (1951) 'The Mechanisms of Age Regression: an Experimental Study', Journal of Abnormal and Social Psychology, 46, 213-225

Orne, M. T. (1959) 'Hypnosis: Artifact and Essence', Journal of Abnormal Psychology, 58, 277-99

Orne, M. T. (1962) 'Hypnotically Induced Hallucinations', in L. J. West, (ed.), Hallucinations, Grune and Stratton, New York, pp. 211-19

Orne, M. T. (1972) 'Can a Hypnotized Subject be Compelled to Carry Out Otherwise Unacceptable Behavior?' International Journal of Clinical and Experimental Hypnosis, 20, 101-17

Orne, M. T. and Evans, F. J. (1966) 'Inadvertent Termination of Hypnosis with Hypnotised and Simulating Subjects', International Journal of Clinical and Experimental Hypnosis, 14, 61-78

Ornstein, R. E. (1969) On the Experience of Time, Penguin Books, Harmondsworth

Perry, C. and Walsh, B. (1978) 'Inconsistencies and Anomalies of Response as a Defining Characteristic of Hypnosis', Journal of Abnormal Psychology, 87, 574-77

Piaget, J. (1971) 'The Child's Conception of Time', Ballantine Books, New York

Posner, M. I. and Snyder, C. R. R. (1975) 'Attention and Cognitive Control', in R. L. Solso (ed.), Information Processing and Cognition: the Loyola Symposium, Erlbaum, Hillsdale, New Jersey

Putnam, W. H. (1979) 'Hypnosis and Distortions in Eyewitness Memory', International Journal of Clinical and Experimental Hypnosis, 27, 437-48

Radford, J. (1974) 'Reflections on Introspection', American Psychologist, 29, 245-50

Redd, W. H. and Andrykowski, M. A. (1982) 'Behavioral Intervention in Cancer Treatment: Controlling Aversive Reactions to Chemotherapy', Journal of Consulting and Clinical Psychology, 50, 1018-29

Reif, R. and Scheerer, M. (1959) Memory and Hypnotic Age Regression: Developmental Aspects of Cognitive Functioning Explored Through Hypnosis, International Universities Press, New York

Reiser, M. and Nielson, M. (1980) 'Investigative Hypnosis: a Developing Speciality', American Journal of Clinical Hypnosis, 23, 75-83

Richardson, A. (1967a) Mental Practice: A Review and Discussion. Part 1, Research Quarterly, 38, 95-107

Richardson, A. (1967b) Mental Practice: A Review and Discussion. Part 2, Research Quarterly, 38, 263-273

Ritterman, M. (1983) Using Hypnosis in Family Therapy, Jossey-Bass Publishers, San Francisco

Rosen, H. (1960) 'Hypnosis - Applications and Misapplications', Journal of the American Medical Association, 172, 139-43

Ross, P. J. (1981) 'Hypnosis as a Counselling Tool', British Journal of Guidance and Counselling, 9, 173-79

Ross, P. J. (1981) 'The Use of Hypnotic Imagery in Vocational Counselling', Bulletin of the British Society of Experimental and Clinical Hypnosis, 4, 22-3

Rousey, C. L. (1961) 'Hypnosis in Speech Pathology and Audiology', Journal of Speech and Hearing Disorders, 26, 258-267

Rowley, D. T. (1984) 'Forensic Hypnosis: Caveats and Proposals', Medicine and Law, 3, 183-91

Ruch, J. C. (1975) 'Self-Hypnosis: The Result of Heterohypnosis or Vice Versa', International Journal of Clinical and Experimental Hypnosis, 23, 282-304

Sacerdote, P. (1970) 'Some Individualized Psychotherapeutic Techniques', International Journal of Clinical and Experimental Hypnosis, 18, 160-80

Sackeim, H. A. (1982) 'Lateral Asymmetry in Bodily Response to Hypnotic Suggestions', Biological Psychiatry, 17, 437-47

St. Jean, R., MacLeod, C., Coe, W. C. and Howard, M. (1982) 'Amnesia and Hypnotic Time Estimation', International Journal of Clinical and Experimental Hypnosis, 30, 127-37

Sanders, R. S. and Reyher, J. (1969) 'Sensory Deprivation and the Enhancement of Hypnotic Susceptibility', Journal of Abnormal Psychology, 74, 375-81

Sarbin, T. R. and Coe, W. C. (1972) Hypnosis: A Social Psychological Analysis of Influence Communication, Holt, Rinehart and Winston, New York

Schneider, W. and Shiffrin, R. M. (1977) 'Controlled and Automatic Information Processing: I. Detection, Search and Attention', Psychological Review, 84, 1-66

Schofield, L. J. and Platoni, K. (1976) 'Manipulation of Visual Imagery under Various Hypnotic Conditions', American Journal of Clinical Hypnosis, 76, 191-99

Sheehan, D. V. and Surman, O. S. (1982) 'Follow-Up Study of Hypnotherapy for Smoking', Journal of the American Society of Psychosomatic Dentistry and Medicine, 29, 1982

Sheehan, P. W. (1973) 'Analysis of the Heterogeneity of 'Faking' and 'Simulating' Performance in the Hypnotic Setting', International Journal of Clinical and Experimental Hypnosis, 21, 213-25

Sheehan, P. W. (1977) 'Incongruity in Trance Behavior: A Defining Property of Hypnosis', Annals of New York Academy of Sciences, 296, pp. 194-207

Sheehan, P. W. and McConkey, K. M. (1982) Hypnosis and Experience: The Exploration of Phenomena and Process, Lawrence Erlbaum Associates, Hillsdale, New Jersey

Sheehan, P. W., Obstoj, I. and McConkey, K. (1976) 'Trance Logic and Cue Structure as Supplied by the Hypnotist', Journal of Abnormal Psychology, 85, 459-472

Sheehan, P. W. and Perry, C. W. (1976) Methodologies of Hypnosis: A Critical Appraisal of Contemporary Paradigms of Hypnosis, Lawrence Erlbaum Associates, Hillsdale, New Jersey

Shelton, T. O. and Mahoney, M. J. (1978) 'The Content and Effect of 'Psyching-up' Strategies in Weight Lifters', Cognitive Therapy and Research, 2, 275-284

Shor, R. E. and Orne, E. C. (1962) Harvard Group Scale of Hypnotic Susceptibility, Consulting Psychologists Press, Palo Alto, California

Sinclair-Gieben, A. H. C. and Chalmers, D. (1959) 'Evaluation of Treatment of Warts by Hypnosis', Lancet, October 3, 480-2

Smith, M. C. (1983) 'Hypnotic Memory Enhancement of Witnesses: Does it Work?', Psychological Bulletin, 94, 387-407

Smith, M. L., Glass, G. V. and Miller, T. I. (1980) The Benefits of Psychotherapy, John Hopkins Press, Baltimore

Snider, G. L. (1978) 'The Treatment of Asthma', The New England Journal of Medicine, 298, 397-99

Sovak, M., Kunzel, M., Sternbach, R. A. and Dalessio, D. J. (1978), 'Is Volitional Manipulation of Hemodynamics a Valid Rationale for Biofeedback Therapy of Migraine?' Headache, 18, 197-202

Spanos, N. P. (1982) 'Hypnotic Behaviour: A Cognitive, Social Psychological Perspective', Research Communications in Psychology, Psychiatry and Behavior, 7, 199-213

Spanos, N. P., Ansari, F. and Stam, H. J. (1979) 'Hypnotic Age Regression and Eidetic Imagery: A Failure to Replicate', Journal of Abnormal Psychology, 88, 88-91

References

Spanos, N. P. and Radtke, H. L. (1982) 'Hypnotic
   Amnesia as Strategic Enactment: A Cognitive,
   Social-Psychological Perspective', Research
   Communuoations in Psychology, Psychiatry and
   Behavior, 7, 215-31
Spanos, N. P., Radtke-Bodorik, H. L., Ferguson, J.
   D. and Jones, B. (1979) 'The Effects of
   Hypnotic Susceptibility, Suggestions for
   Analgesia, and the Utilization of Cognitive
   Strategies on the Reduction of Pain', Journal
   of Abnormal Psychology, 88, 282-92
Spanos, N. P., Weekes, J. R. and De Groh, M. (1984)
   'The "Involuntary" Countering of Suggested
   Requests: A Test of the Ideomotor Hypothesis of
   Hypnotic Responsiveness', British Journal of
   Experimental and Clinical Hypnosis, 1, 3-11
Spiegel, H. (1976) Manual for Hypnotic Induction
   Profile: Eye-roll Levitation Method, (rev.
   ed.), Soni-Medica, New York
Spiegel, H. (1977) 'The Hypnotic Induction Profile
   (HIP): A Review of its Development', Annals of
   New York Academy of Sciences, 296, 129-42
Spiegel, H. and Spiegel, D. (1978) Trance and
   Treatment: Clinical Uses of Hypnosis, Basic
   Books, New York
Stanton, H. E. (1976) 'Fee-paying and Weight Loss:
   Evidence for an Interesting Reaction', American
   Journal of Clinical and Experimental Hypnosis,
   26, 22-9
Stanton, H. E. (1981) 'Maximizing the Placebo Effect
   in the Treatment of Demoralized Patients',
   Australian Journal of Clinical and Experimental
   Hypnosis, 9, 87-92
Starker, S. (1974) 'Effects of Hypnotic Induction
   upon Visual Imagery', Journal of Nervous Mental
   Disorders, 159, 433-437
Stein, C. (1963) 'The Clenched Fist Technique as a
   Hypnotic Procedure in Clinical Psychotherapy',
   American Journal of Clinical Hypnosis, 6,
   113-19
Stern, D. B., Spiegel, H. and Nee, J. C. M. (1979)
   'The Hypnotic Induction Profile: Normative
   Observations, Reliability and Validity',
   Journal of Clinical Hypnosis, 21, 109-33
Sternbach, R. A. (1968) Pain: A Psychophysiological
   Analysis, Academic Press, New York
Tart, C. T. (1969) (ed.), Altered States of
   Consciousness, John Wiley and Sons Inc., New
   York

Tart, C. T. (1970) 'Self-report Scales of Hypnotic Depth', International Journal of Clinical and Experimental Hypnosis, 18, 105-25

Tart, C. T. (1972) 'Measuring the Depth of an Altered Scale of Consciousness, with Special Reference to Self-Report Scales of Hypnotic Depth' in E. Fromm and R. E. Shor (eds.), Hypnosis: Developments in Research and New Perspectives, Aldine-Atherton, New York, pp. 445-477

Tart, C. T. (1978) 'Quick and Convenient Assessment of Hypnotic Depth: Self-report Scales', American Journal of Clinical Hypnosis, 21, 186-207

Tart, C. T. (1979) 'Measuring the Depth of an Altered State of Consciousness, with Particular Reference to Self-Report Scales of Hypnotic Depth' in E. From and R. E. Shor (eds.), Hypnosis; Developments in Research and New Perspectives, Aldine Publishing Company, New York, pp. 567-601

Tellegen, A. and Atkinson, G. (1974) 'Openness to Absorbing and Self-Altering Experiences ("absorption"), a Trait Related to Hypnotic Susceptibility', Journal of Abnormal Psychology, 83, 268-77

Thornton, E. M. (1976) Hypnotism, Hysteria and Epilepsy: An Historical Synthesis, Heinemann, London

Tulving, E. (1972) 'Episodic and Semantic Memory', in E. Tulving and W. Donaldson, (eds.), Organization of Memory, Academic Press, New York, pp. 590-600

Udolf, R. (1981) Handbook of Hypnosis for Professionals, Van Nostrand Reinhold Company, New York

Underwood, G. and Stevens, R. (1979) (eds.), Aspects of Consciousness, vol. 1, Psychological Issues, Academic Press, London

Underwood, G. and Stevens, R. (1981) (eds.), Aspects of Consciousness, vol. 2, Structural Issues, Academic Press, London

Underwood, H. W. (1960) 'The Validity of Hypnotically Induced Visual Hallucinations', Journal of Abnormal and Social Psychology, 61, 39-46

Vingoe, F. J. (1968a) 'The Development of a Group Alert Trance Scale', International Journal of Clinical and Experimental Hypnosis, 16, 120-32

References

Vingoe, F. J. (1968b) 'The Utilization of a Group Alert-Trance Technique in Facilitating Human Performance', Paper Presented at the Meeting of the Western Psychological Association, San Diego, California

Vingoe, F. J. (1973) 'Comparison of the Harvard Group Scale of Hypnotic Susceptibility, Form A and the Group Alert Trance Scale in a University Population', The International Journal of Clinical and Experimental Hypnosis, 21, 169-79

Wadden, T. A. and Anderton, C. H. (1982) 'The Clinical Use of Hypnosis', Psychological Bulletin, 91, 215-243

Wadden, T. A. and Penrod, J. H. (1981) 'Hypnosis in the Treatment of Alcoholism: a Review' American Journal of Clinical Hypnosis, 24, 41-7

Wagstaff, G. F. (1981) Hypnosis, Compliance and Belief, The Harvester Press, Brighton

Wagstaff, G. F. (1984) 'The Enhancement of Witness Memory by 'Hypnosis': a Review and Methodological Critique of the Experimental Literature', British Journal of Experimental and Clinical Hypnosis, 2, 3-12

Wagstaff, G. F. and Ovenden, M. (1979) 'Hypnotic Time Distortion and Free-Recall Learning - An Attempted Replication', Psychological Research, 40, 291-8

Wagstaff, G. F., Traverse, J. and Milner, S. (1982) 'Hypnosis and Eyewitness Memory: Two Experimental Analogues', IRCS Medical Science, 10, 894-5

Walker, L. G. (1984a) 'Aversions to Chemotherapy in Patients with Lymphoid Tumours', Proceedings of the First Annual Conference of the British Society of Experimental and Clinical Hypnosis, pp. 86-92

Walker, L. G. (1984b) 'Irritable Bowel Syndrome: Two Case Studies', Proceedings of the First Annual Conference of the British Society of Experimental and Clinical Hypnosis, pp. 46-52

Wallace, B. (1978) 'Restoration of Eidetic Imagery Via Hypnotic Age Regression: More Evidence', Journal of Abnormal Psychology, 87, 673-5

Waters, W. E. and O'Connor, P. J. (1971) 'Epidemiology of Headache in Women', Journal of Neurology, Neurosurgery and Psychiatry, 34, 148-53

Watkins, J. G (1947) 'Antisocial Compulsions Induced Under Hypnotic Trance', Journal of Abnormal and Social Psychology, 42, 256-9

181

Weitzenhoffer, A. M. (1972) 'Behavior Therapeutic Techniques and Hypnotherapeutic Methods', American Journal of Clinical Hypnosis, 15, 71-82

Weitzenhoffer, A. M. (1978a) 'Hypnotism and Altered States of Consciousness', in A. Sugarman and R. E. Tarter (eds.), Expanding Dimensions of Consciousness, Springer, New York

Weitzenhoffer, A. M. (1978b) 'What Did He (Bernheim) Say?' in F. H. Frankel and H. S. Zamansky (eds.), Hypnosis at its Bicentennial, Plenum, New York

Weitzenhoffer, A. M. and Hilgard, E. R. (1959) Stanford Hypnotic Susceptibility Scale Forms A and B, Consulting Psychologists Press, Palo Alto, California

Weitzenhoffer, A. M. and Hilgard, E. R. (1962) Stanford Hypnotic Susceptibility Scale Form C, Consulting Psychologists Press, Palo Alto, California

Weitzenhoffer, A. M. and Hilgard, E. R. (1967) Revised Stanford Profile Scales of Hypnotic Susceptibility, Forms I and II, Consulting Psychologists Press, Palo Alto, California

White, R. W. (1941) 'A Preface to a Theory of Hypnotism', Journal of Abnormal and Social Psychology', 36, 477-505

Wickramasekera, I. (1973) 'Effects of Electromyographic Feedback on Hypnotic Susceptibility: More Preliminary Data', Journal of Abnormal Psychology, 83, 74-7

Wilkinson, J. B. (1984) 'Autohypnosis in the Treatment of Anxiety with Special Reference to Hyperventilation', Proceedings of the First Annual Conference of the British Society of Experimental and Clinical Hypnosis, pp. 78-84

Wilson, S. C. and Barber, T. X. (1978) 'The Creative Imagination Scale as a Measure of Hypnotic Responsiveness: Applications to Experimental and Clinical Hypnosis', American Journal of Clinical Hypnosis, 20, 235-49

Wilson, S. C. and Barber, T. X. (1982) 'The Fantasy-prone Personality: Implications for Understanding Imagery, Hypnosis and Parapsychological Phenomena', in A. A. Sheikh (ed.), Imagery: Current Theory, Research and Application, Wiley, New York

Wolpe, J. (1958) Psychotherapy by Reciprocal Inhibition, Stanford University Press, Stanford

Young, J. and Cooper, L. M. (1972) 'Hypnotic Recall
    Amnesia as a Function of Manipulated
    Expectancy', <u>Proceedings of 80th Annual
    Convention of American Psychological
    Association</u>, <u>7</u>, 857-88
Young, P. C. (1952) 'Antisocial Uses of Hypnosis',
    in L. M. LeCron (ed.), <u>Experimental Hypnosis</u>,
    Macmillan Publishing Company Inc., New York,

Sheehan, D. V. 136
Sheehan, P. W. 19, 48,
  61, 84, 85
  133, 135
Shelton, T. O. 145
Shiffrin, R. M. 27
Shor, R. E. 38, 48
Simon, H. A. 24
Sinclair-Gieben, A. H. C.
  124
Singer, J. L. 143
Smith, J. R. 84
Smith, M. C. 91, 156
Smith, M. L. 99
Snider, G. L. 116
Snyder, C. R. R. 27
Sovak, M. 127
Spanos, N. P. 21, 22, 23,
  45, 88, 95, 97, 132
Spiegel, D. 40, 49, 100
Spiegel, H. E. 40, 49,
  50, 66
Stam, H. J. 88
Stanton, H. E. 126, 129
Starker, S. 88
Stein, C. 79, 116, 136
Stern, D. B. 49
Sternbach, R. A. 127, 132
Stevens, R. 38, 39
Surman, O. S. 136

Tart, C. T. 16, 29, 30,
  38, 39, 74
Tellegen, A. 56
Tewell, K. 119
Thornton, E. M. 4
Traverse, J. 156
Tryon, W. W. 50
Tulving, E. 94

Udolf, R. 4, 13, 40, 43,
  48, 50, 61, 67, 76,
  80, 82, 94, 97, 101,
  114, 121, 133, 146,
  147, 151, 157, 161
Underwood, G. 38, 39
Underwood, H. W. 83

Van Helmont 2
Vellios, A. T. 50

Vingoe, F. J. 49, 71
Von Bosch, A. 3

Wadden, T. A. 99, 113,
  115, 116, 123, 129
Wagstaff, G. F. 16, 18,
  22, 23, 25, 45, 53,
  54, 55, 57, 59, 77,
  87, 91, 94, 94, 97,
  156
Wakely, T. 7
Walker, L. G. 119, 125
Wall, P. D. 132
Wallace, B. 88
Walsh, B. 89
Waters, W. E. 127
Watkins, J. G. 153
Weekes, J. R. 45
Weitzenhoffer, A. M. 50,
  51, 52, 103
White, R. W. 14
Wickramasekera, I. 54
Wilkinson, J. B. 115
Wilson, S. C. 18, 48, 88
Wolpe, J. 104
Worring, R. W. 155

Young, P. C. 93, 153

meta-analysis 99
therapeutic techniques
100-112
 abreaction 135
 analytic psychotherapy
 101-103
 aversive therapy 106-
 107, 129
 behaviour therapy 103,
 122, 135
 brief hypnotherapy
 107-109
 counselling 109
 covert desensitisation
 113
 covert sensitisation
 107
 dissociation 134
 distraction techniques
 133
 ego-strengthening 117,
 126, 145, 146
 family therapy 109-11
 flooding 105-106
 focusing 134
 glove anaesthesia 128,
 133
 hypnodrama 111-12
 hypnosis 100-101
 symptom amelioration
 109
 symptom substitution
 107-108
 symptom transformation
 108
 symptom utilization
 109
 systematic
 desensitisation 104-
 105, 115, 135
 time distortion 122,
 134
theories 23-24
torticollis 130
time distortion 85-87
trance 14-15, 19
trance depth 16
trance logic 83-85

uterine bleeding 126

viruses 123-24
voice disorders 137

warts 123-24

Zoist 7, 8